Wednesday's Women

IOll5908

(Women Writers In New Zealand 1945-1970)

Dr Michael O'Leary

Earl of Seacliff Art Workshop
Paekakariki
2015

Anne McCahon was 'the best artist of her generation'
      Dunedin set-designer Rodney Kennedy
'Colin [McCahon] overcame his only real artistic rival by marrying her'
      William McCahon

Wednesday's Women was originally written as a thesis for the degree of Doctor of Philosophy in Gender and Women's Studies, Victoria University of Wellington.
The academic title is:
'Social and Literary Constraints on Women Writers in New Zealand: 1945-1970'.

Wednesday's Women is published by
ESAW
PO Box 42
Paekakariki 5034

ISBN: 978-1-86942-163-2

Contents

Acknowledgements

I want to acknowledge and thank my supervisors for my PhD thesis on which this book is based: Alison Laurie and Prue Hyman from the Gender and Women's Studies Department of Victoria University, Wellington, along with Lesley Hall, all of whom supported the idea for this thesis from the time I first proposed it. I also acknowledge the assistance and support of private scholars Dr. F.W.N. Wright, Rowan Gibbs, and Mark Pirie who provided me with much unpublished and privately published work, as well as their comments on many aspects of this work. I would like to thank Wellington bookseller John Quilter, who alerted me to much arcane and out of print material on the subject of my thesis, as did Peter Trewern from New Zealand Book Auctions. I thank the Poetry Archive of New Zealand Aotearoa. I would also like to thank my friends and whānau for their on-going support. Lastly, I want to thank all the women, friends and lovers, who over my 60 years on earth have cared for me and been part of my life.

This book is dedicated to the memory of our parents Maurice and Patricia O'Leary who both died in 1968. The last song mum sang to me went: 'Hey Jude, don't make it bad; Take a sad song and make it better'. It is also dedicated to our sister, Cathleen, who died in 1954 aged 22 months.

Foreword by Prue Hyman

It is a great pleasure to write a short tribute to Michael O'Leary and his work to document and explain the extreme neglect, adverse criticism and/or trivialization of the work of New Zealand women writers in the 1945/70 period. When I was approached to act as a joint supervisor for his Victoria University doctoral thesis on this topic, I was doubtful, fearing that my feminist economics expertise was insufficiently central to the project. And perhaps I was initially a shade uncertain about a man writing this particular thesis! However, I am very glad to have been persuaded that I could be useful, adding context to the specific literary side where Alison Laurie would provide major assistance.

Raised in England and with a limited knowledge of the women writers Michael was discussing, I learned a lot (as supervisors often do!) – and he was a pleasure to supervise. His extensive background as a reader, author, publisher, bookseller, and social justice advocate with unique access to unpublished material and literary figures of the time equipped him wonderfully to write this thesis and book. Michael's own writing includes 5 novels and several volumes of poetry and short stories, as well as non-fiction. His Earl of Seacliff Art Workshop imprint has published over 120 titles of New Zealand literary works over 28 years. He has clearly put his money where his mouth is - of the 61 authors published in its first 25 years, 26 were women writers – I have enjoyed several recent launches of books under his imprint by local women authors such as Annabel Fagan and Frances Cherry.

This book clearly establishes the anti women biases of the male literary establishment of this period, showing how Allan Curnow's Modernist school of thought echoed T.S. Eliot's 'ban on the personal' and dominated the Georgian school. His evidence is sufficient "to show a definite trend, and at times specific deliberate examples, of male indifference and at times malevolence directed towards female subjects, sensibilities and styles of writing as well as individual women writers themselves." His case studies are fascinating and provoke an appetite for more. So some readers may well want to go to the thesis itself, which is on line, to read the detailed appendices with bibliographies of selected women authors, together with fascinating correspondence and reviews which flesh out the book even further. They also contain material on the reclamation of many of the women writers by second wave feminists and include an interesting interview with poet Heather McPherson from the Spiral publishing collective.

Michael points out interesting differences between the treatment of women novelists of the time and women poets. The novelists were, in the main, ignored by the literary world, though many, such as Ngaio Marsh, Dorothy Eden, and Dorothy Quentin, published successfully overseas. Meanwhile the poets, particularly Eileen Duggan, were not ignored, but instead treated "with a mixture of disdain and hostility". Michael puts his work in context, with discussion of the economic, social and historical context, including the impact of the Second World War. He covers the Rosie the Riveter effect which pushed women back to the home until increasing labour demand together with women's education and desire to re-enter public life led to major change throughout society, including the literary world. Do read this book!

Chapter 1

Introduction

This book explores the reasons why so few women writers in New Zealand appear as prominent figures in the literary scene during the period from the end of World War Two up to the time when the second wave of the New Zealand feminist movement began, in the late 1960s and early 1970s. It discusses whether women writers were deliberately under-represented and their work trivialised by the male writers and publishers of the time. If so, what were the factors accounting for this under-representation?

I provide an overview of the women writers and their acceptance or otherwise in New Zealand literature from 1945 to 1970, based on an investigation of the literary world of the time, plus one example from the art world which in many respects is similar in attitude and underlying conditions. This includes an examination of the evidence regarding the extent to which many New Zealand women writers felt excluded or belittled by their male counterparts and their analysis of the reasons for this – together with discussion of the accuracy of their perceptions. What are the factors accounting for their seeming lack of representation and how significant is each?

To what extent were there successes and achievements, literary, commercial, and academic, for the women writers of the time, despite any real or perceived exclusions? The dates selected are significant for it was in 1945 that Allen Curnow's anthology of New Zealand verse appeared for the first time. One of the striking things about the collection is that only two of the sixteen poets, Robin Hyde and Ursula Bethell, represented are women. Curnow's book went into a second edition in 1951 with twenty men and three women included, Ruth Dallas being the third. Were more women asked to contribute to the anthology but refused and, if so, why?

Subsidiary questions relate to specific issues and groups of women writers. The year 1945 saw the end of WW2 and the return of many thousands of servicemen to New Zealand from Europe. Did their return also mean a return to traditional family gender roles, not just in the home but also outside the domestic situation, including the literary world? Was there a residual resentment held by the men returning from the war towards the women who stayed at home, and did such attitudes also cross over into the post-war literary environment? Beyond individual women writers there is evidence to suggest that in the period 1945 to 1970, different groups of women were treated differently, or simply ignored as being 'other', in particular, Māori women writers and lesbian writers.

One of the motivations for me to write this book came from a previous publication of mine. The subject for that study was small press publishing in New Zealand from 1969 to 1999, published by Wellington publishers Steele Roberts in 2007. My introductory chapter outlined some of the history of New Zealand literature as printed word up to 1969. What struck me was the under-representation of women writers in the period before the 1970s, according to most of the literary commentators. However, I knew this to be untrue because of my many years as a second-hand bookseller. I realised this was an area that needed further investigation, and that the questions raised in my book signalled a direction for important new research.

The time period of this present book ends in 1970, so does not cover the explosion of energy running through the 1970s in what is often referred to as Second Wave Feminism. Yoko Ono in her 1972 song 'Sisters o sisters' brought into popular culture some of the frustrations and sentiments that women were feeling at the time:

We lost our green land, we lost our clean air,
We lost our true wisdom and we live in despair.
O sisters, o sisters, let's stand up right now,
it's never too late to start from the start
(Ono, 1972: song lyric).

During this period of the early 1970s women in New Zealand began to 'start from the start' with the Women's Art Movement that set up art galleries, holding their own exhibitions so they were no longer reliant on gallery owners and art dealers who were predominantly men. At the same time women writers established publishing houses and bookshops, no longer reliant on the male publishers. These responses in New Zealand and elsewhere came as a reaction to the treatment of women during the period of this study 1945 to 1970 and changed the position of women writers.

Another more recent event which made me want to write on this topic was the twentieth anniversary of Keri Hulme's *The Bone People* winning the Booker Prize, the only New Zealand book to have done so. A symposium was held to celebrate this achievement at Victoria University and apart from myself, none of the male university literary academics, VUP writers or other male writers in the Wellington region turned up to honour Hulme. When I asked writer and academic Lydia Wevers, one of the conference organisers, what she thought about this situation she told me that they had certainly been invited. As, despite this, they did not attend, I concluded that the silencing of the 'other' (in the case of women, half the population) continues despite such international success.

While there has been a body of published work on New Zealand women writers in recent years, including those of the period I am investigating, such work is to a greater or lesser extent deficient in feminist critique. It does, however, provide the raw material for such a critique. Thus I also investigate the sociological, economic, class, racial, and cultural pressures which either hindered or encouraged women writers, including norms related to gender division of labour within families and their impact on women's opportunities to put writing at the centre of their lives. In particular, several of these issues are investigated in Chapter 3 which addresses the social and historical themes. The issues relating to Māori women writers are discussed in Chapter 8.

The book looks at the apparent marginalisation of women writers by male writers, critics and publishers. One example I will in some depth involved the poet Ruth Gilbert. In 1957 the literary magazine *numbers* published a letter by Willow Macky in which she 'criticises the critics' of the New Zealand literary scene, as will be discussed in the study of the poets in Chapter 5. Gilbert, whose work sparked this controversy, will be examined in some detail. There were also some interesting marriages between creative people during this period, for example, poets James K. Baxter and J.C. Sturm, Meg and Alistair Campbell, and artists Anne and Colin McCahon.

I examine the work of Māori women writing in English during the period, in particular the works published in *Te Ao Hou*, including waiata and reviews. For example, J.C. Sturm was writing book reviews and Arapera Blank short stories. The waiata of women such as Rangi Dewes and Erihapeti Murchie, whose husband has given me access to her unpublished waiata, and the influence of Māori women's writing on cultural and sociological subjects is also relevant during this period and is explored. Having access to unpublished written material has allowed this study to discover women writers' stories that may have gone unrecognised. In Murchie's case it is doubtful that her writing would have been accessible beyond her whānau. In the case of Renée and Karen Butterworth, had I not encouraged them to contribute their stories these may have not have become available until either of them wrote a memoir. I hope this will encourage them to do so.

The book investigates lesbian writing, whether identified either explicitly or implicitly, among the women writers of the time. Academic, Aorewa McLeod, reminds us: 'Mander, Marsh, Escott, and in the art world Hodgkins, all lived before second wave feminism and gay liberation came to New Zealand in the early 1970s and made lesbian visibility possible'. In this chapter it is argued that writing by women who dealt with lesbian themes was unacknowledged as such by the publishing and critical literary establishment; where acknowledged, these writers were not published or recognised in the 1945-70 period. The reason that most of the lesbian writers in this chapter are from outside the 1945-70 period highlights the fact that lesbian writing and lifestyles were not written of during this time. Heather Murray in *The Oxford Companion to New Zealand Literature* on the 'New Zealand Writer's Conference, 1951' writes:

> regardless of which men were in or out [of favour], nearly all women were out. Between Author's Week 1936, which celebrated a mainly female creative literature, and 1951, women's writing had been demoted by the middle generation of male writers as trivial, irrelevant or ill-disciplined. As literary arbiters, editors (Brasch), critics (Bertram, Curnow, Brasch), publishers and printers (Glover and Caxton), and compilers of influential anthologies (Curnow), this generation shaped the course literature was to take until the 1970s. Only then did women's writing begin its hard-fought move back in from the margins (Murray, 1998: 406).

A metaphorical undercurrent to this work is provided in *A Room of One's Own* by Virginia Woolf, which imagines Shakespeare having a sister who is also a gifted writer. Woolf writes of the short-lived attempts of 'Judith' Shakespeare to employ her talents in the same way as her famous brother. This may also say something about the New Zealand women who could perhaps have been writers during the period. The women I have included in my study did at least manage to get published – there are undoubtedly others, who, like Judith Shakespeare, did not even manage to get started.

While it is outside the scope of this work it is important to note here that some of the New Zealand women writers who were successful during the period 1945-70 found success overseas. I conclude this introduction with a quote from Woolf in which she states the situation women are often perceived to be observed from and which view underpins this study:

> but women feel just as men feel; they need exercise for their faculties and a field for their efforts ... they suffer from too rigid a restraint, too absolute a stagnation, precisely as men would suffer; and it is narrow-minded in their privileged fellow-creatures [that is, men] to say that they ought to confine themselves to making puddings and knitting stockings, to playing on the piano and embroidering bags. It is thoughtless to condemn them, or laugh at them, if they seek to do more or learn more than custom has pronounced necessary for their sex (Woolf, 2000: 89).

Chapter 2

Feminist methodology

It has been important in understanding the issues raised in the book to provide a feminist background. Thus, the methodology underpinning this study is based on feminist theory. I examine the views expressed at the time by the women writers themselves and accord their views the status of material evidence rather than dismissing these as subjective opinion. My study also draws upon a range of feminist literature and ideas. In particular, my approach is informed by the ideas of Shulamit Reinharz (1992), Gayle Letherby (2003), Adrienne Rich (2001) and Linda Tuhiwai Smith (1992). My work is essentially an attempt to 'salvage from the wreck' (Rich) an understanding of an era in our literature in which many women writers were unacknowledged simply because they were women.

Feminist theory is concerned with sexism in any given society, and asks how does the theory describe and understand the position of women in society? What are the sources of women's oppression and who gains from negative stereotyping of women? Researching a wide range of feminist research methods Reinharz (1992) explains the relationship between feminism and methodology and challenges existing stereotypes. She concludes there is no one correct feminist method, but rather a variety of perspectives and argues that such a diversity of methods has been of great value to feminist scholarship. Australian feminist writer Renate Klein states:

> An emerging postulate for feminist - is using a variety of methods to generate multifaceted information (Klein in Reinharz, 1992: 197).

Among the 'Multiple Methods' suggested by Reinharz that are relevant to the literature based thesis I am presenting are 'Commitment to Thoroughness' and 'Integration of the Personal and the Social', which in my case also includes interface with the literary information of the women's own writing, and the 'Quest Image' which entails the 'quest' for the truth behind the 'known facts'. This approach is particularly pertinent to my way of 'looking' at the subject due to my own involvement in literature as a writer and publisher who is seen as being outside the literary 'establishment'.

Feminist literary criticism looks at literary works and their creators differently from much traditional criticism which has tended to see works of literature in an hierarchical, comparative, judgemental and what claims to be 'objective' manner. However, as Elaine Showalter points out in her introduction to her edited collections of early feminist criticism:

> Since the late 1960s, when feminist criticism developed as part of the international women's movement, the assumptions of literary study have been profoundly altered. Whereas it had always been taken for granted that the representative reader, writer, and critic of Western literature is male, feminist criticism has shown that women readers and critics bring different perceptions and expectations to their literary experience, and has insisted that women have also told important stories of our culture (Showalter, 1985: 3).

While Showalter is an American academic, the fact that New Zealand generally comes under the banner of 'Western culture' means that her analysis of the situation of women's writing can be adapted to the New Zealand cultural and literary climate. The period this thesis deals with ends roughly at the time Showalter regards as being 'part of the international women's movement', that is the late 1960s and early 1970s, which illustrates the relevance of that change and coincides with the loosening of the traditional and sexist attitudes which dominated literary and cultural life for New Zealand women writers before the 'liberation'. In her essay, 'Feminist Criticism in the Wilderness', Showalter investigates the question also posed by many of the New Zealand women writers in this study, that is: what exactly is feminine or women's writing? She discusses Virginia Woolf and Hèléne Cixous, who take differing positions to this question. Woolf discusses feminine perspective by stating:

> A woman's writing is always feminine, it can't help being feminine; at its best it is most feminine; the only difficulty lies in defining what we mean by feminine (Woolf in Showalter, 1985: 247).

However, Cixous thinks it cannot be defined:

> It is impossible to define a feminine practice of writing, and this is an impossibility that will remain, for this practice will never be theorized, enclosed, encoded – which doesn't mean that it doesn't exist (Cixous in Showalter, 1985: 247-8).

Much of my argument inherent in this study revolves around the question of how so many of the women writers in New Zealand in the period 1945 to 1970 also 'did not exist' in terms of the N.Z. literary world's recognition.

Gayle Letherby argues that there is no such thing as a 'feminist method' but rather a 'feminist methodology' – one which is respectful of respondents and acknowledges the subjective involvement of the researcher, using the word 'I' rather than 'One'. New Zealand academic, Alison Jones, in discussing the objective versus subjective approach to academic writing, argues that the orthodox view on knowledge has been changed by postmodernists and feminists, and points out that the 'I' is central and people's accounts of the world are constructions, made up from the language, meanings and ideas historically available to them as the 'I'. This is significant to my approach, due to my own involvement in the literary world.

The concept of 'Otherness' is discussed and suggests that the lack of proportion in power relationships is central to the construction of 'otherness'. Only the dominant group is in a position to impose the value of its particularity and to devalue the particularity of 'others' while also imposing discriminatory measures on the 'Other'. French existentialist philosopher Simone de Beauvoir's example, that if the Other of 'Man' is 'Woman', and if 'Man' is the dominant group, this indicates that women's secondary political, legal, and economic status relative to men, are evident in myths such as the Biblical tale of creation where God creates Adam first and Eve second, as Adam's companion.

According to de Beauvoir, male-dominated cultures represent humanity as male and define woman as relative to man. Woman, while not a minority numerically, is the 'Other', an object reflective of men's desires and fears. Women, as an oppressed caste, are forced to accommodate themselves to this identity, denying their own freedom. The domestic confinement of women can be analysed as reducing the woman to her domestic role, that patriarchal society creates and reproduces gender inequality. In *The Second Sex* de Beauvoir argued that women must counter these myths with phenomenological descriptions of their own lived experience and challenge their secondary status in a political struggle for women's liberation. In this she was prophetic, and by the end of the period covered by this book, the late 1960s and into the 1970s and beyond, third wave feminism had brought de Beauvoir's ideas and ideals into reality.

Otherness also equals a form of binarism: that is the opposition of colonist/native or White/of Colour, Man/Woman. For example, in his book

Orientalism, Edward Said states that the West/Orient duality encompasses all of the components of Otherness. The Oriental is characterized by his barbarity, his savageness and his race. The Orient is the geographical fiction that gives him geographical basis. Orientalism is the discourse through which the West constructs the Otherness of the Turks, Moroccans, Persians, Indians, Japanese: all reduced to the same stigmatizing stereotypes, and thus gives itself an identity in opposition to them.

However, taking Said's ideas further, not all forms of Otherness are fully (or even mainly) geographical in nature. Women, homosexuals and the insane, all major figures of Otherness in the West, owe their stigmatization to something other than their location. Aspects of these forms of 'Otherness' are also discussed. For example, Māori writer Linda Tuhiwai Smith is concerned not only with colonialism and its effect on Māori traditional society, but how Otherness in the racial sense does not necessarily sit well with Otherness in the sexual sense, that is, in the context of Pākehā feminism. The Otherness of Janet Frame is discussed in Chapter 6 and the particular form of Otherness that is lesbianism in Chapter 9 in relation to lesbian writers in New Zealand.

Dominated groups in society are Others precisely because they are subject to the categories and practices of the dominant in-group and because they are unable to prescribe their own norms. However, women represent a particularly singular type of Out-group. Not because they are numerically less in number than the dominant group, but because of their sex alone. Out-groups cease to be Others when they manage to escape the oppression forced upon them by in-groups, in other words, when they succeed in conferring upon themselves a positive, autonomous identity. It is, therefore, one of my aims to facilitate this idea - if the women writers of the 1945 to 1970 period in New Zealand can be considered in terms of their Otherness to New Zealand male writers of the time.

However, any chapter on Māori women writers from the period, for example, will have difficulties due to the paucity of written and published literature available. Also, in adopting a feminist critique it will be seen that feminist methodologies and studies arose from the thinking of 'white women', which may not necessarily fit into a Māori perspective. As Māori academic, Tuhiwai Smith, points out that when Māori women control their own definitions the fundamental unit of identity which can make sense of different realities lies in whakapapa, and this 'reality' can often be in conflict with theoretical ideas about how things should be. The position of Māori poet J.C. Sturm provides one example of the difficulties faced by Māori women writers during this period.

Post-colonial literature often involves writings that deal with issues of de-colonization or the political and cultural independence of people formerly subjected to colonial rule. It is also a literary critique of texts that carry racist or colonial undertones, as similarly feminist literary critique identifies sexist undertones. According to New Zealand academic, Patrick Evans, the New Zealand that began to thaw and stir in the early 1970s had been mono-cultural for more than 50 years. It could also be said that the literary world in New Zealand from the 1940s to the 1970s could be described as having been 'mono-sexual' and I draw that aspect of the New Zealand 'blokes' literary culture out and to ask: where are the women, and why aren't they there?

Post-colonialism and feminism both investigate particular instances in human culture where one conceptual thread that links all its various interpretations is the rejection of universalism, which refers to the notion of a unitary and homogeneous human nature. Angeli R. Diaz, for example, writes that particular to feminist theory is postcolonial theory's rejection of universalism that resonates with the Third Wave feminist agenda of inclusiveness. So, while terms like post-modern, post-colonial, multi-culturalism and others were not in wide use during the 1945-1970 period they do impact in retrospect.

My approach is also influenced by feminist economic and social theory based on a Marxist feminist and materialist framework. I do not seek to evaluate the texts from the perspective of literary theory, rather I ask what were the circumstances of their production, that is, what were the constraints inhibiting the ability of the women writers to produce work during the period, and who owned the means of producing books, that is, who owned the presses, thus controlling the so-called freedom of the press. For example, my approach is informed by the insights of feminist economist Prue Hyman (1994). Thus, women's economic and social status was affected by the pervading gender and family norms of the time and this influenced their ability to firstly produce their work and then to get it published by the owners of the publishing houses at the time. As Terry Eagleton writes in *Marxism and Literary Criticism*:

> Literature may be an artefact, a product of social consciousness, a world vision; but it is also an *industry*. Books are not just structures of meaning, they are also commodities produced by publishers and sold on the market for profit ... Critics are not just analysts of texts: they are also (usually) academics hired by the state to prepare students ideologically for their functions within capitalist society. Writers are not just transposers of trans-individual mental structures, they are also workers hired by publishing houses to produce commodities which will sell (Eagleton, 1985: 59).

I also examine the economic concerns of the time in relation to the publishing and retail book industry, informed by feminist economic theory. One of the issues for feminist publishers was whether to publish for a mass market or not. It will be noted that several women in this study wrote to make a living, either as journalists or writers of popular fiction, and this was often in conflict with those who wanted a more philosophical-theoretical approach to women's literature. For example, in a chapter on 'Women's Publishers', the authors of *Rolling our own* quote the 'Onlywomen Press':

> In order to create a Women's Liberation Movement reality, we need discussion and the development of political analysis unhindered by patriarchal values. We need a means of establishing our own culture (Onlywomen Press in Cadman, Chester & Pivot, 1981: 29). [the authors then continue] Feminist publishing, more than any other aspect of the book production process [including the writing], seems to epitomise most clearly the problems and choices which face feminists confronted with a society which is both patriarchal and capitalistic (Cadman, Chester & Pivot, 1981: 29).

Thus, feminist publishing is faced with two of the classical Marxist propositions: who owns and controls the means of production, and who benefits? Most of the women in this study had little choice. If they wanted to write and sell books they had to go with the big commercial companies, but as Cadman, Chester and Pivot point out, this approach:

> almost certainly means watering down the content of the books, and having decisions about style of presentation, publicity and promotion and so on decided for them. The main advantage is that their books will, potentially, have a wider audience, since larger companies have greater resources (Cadman, Chester & Pivot, 1981: 41).

This certainly had ramifications for the writers of romance and so-called light fiction, several of whom reacted with self-deprecating humour; Rosemary Rees, for example, ruefully pointed out that she was New Zealand's best selling author.

This underlying conundrum can be illustrated by a case study of a well-educated and motivated woman, 'Betty', in a feminist account of women and the economic and social change brought about by World War II, *Rosie the Riveter Revisited*. Feminist author Sherna Gluck describes the situation of women in her own country, some of which is relevant when considering pre-1970s attitudes towards women experienced by many of the New Zealand women writers featuring in my study. Gluck writes of Betty:

> She certainly chafed at any suggestion that she was less able because she was a woman. But women like Betty have had few outlets to express their anger [at being treated less than equally than men because they are women]. Their 'premature feminism' could not take root without a social movement to support it (Gluck, 1988: 105).

The term 'Rosie the Riveter' was first used in 1942 in a song of the same name written by Redd Evans and John Jacob Loeb. The song was recorded by many artists and became a nationwide hit in the U.S.A. It tells the story of 'Rosie', a tireless assembly line worker doing her bit for the American war effort. While real-life 'Rosie the Riveters' took on previously male dominated jobs during the war, women in the U.S.A. were often expected to return to household work when the soldiers returned from overseas. Similar occurrences took place in post-war New Zealand after World War Two. For example, in Brian Edwards' biography of New Zealand Prime Minister, Helen Clark, Edwards points out that for Clark's mother:

> There was heavy competition for jobs. Servicemen who had returned from the War and gone to Training College were given the first option on teaching positions as they came up. Margaret [Clark's mother] found it difficult to find a job anywhere near home and she and her friends applied for positions in the most unlikely places (Edwards, 2001: 32).

This is one example that illustrates some of the difficulties that many women faced gaining employment after the war, a situation I see as affecting many women writers of the post-war period. Though there were organisations campaigning for women's equal rights during the period between what is regarded as first and second wave feminism it would be difficult to argue that such groups had the broad grassroots appeal that post-1970s Women's Liberation groups had, or large events such as the United Women's Conference.

Groups such as the Equal Pay Campaign and the efforts of unionists to improve working conditions for women, and organisations like Family Planning seeking to limit excessive pregnancies and the promotion of contraception, were not broadly based. Therefore they were unlikely to attract large numbers of women or to directly provide women with the sense of solidarity and support that developed in the post-1970s period. In Chapter 7 poet Karen Butterworth's contribution also touches on these issues in relation to the public service and brings them into context. The relevance of the pre-feminist 1970s and the lack of 'a social movement' to support the women writers who are investigated in this study is also a recurring theme throughout the years 1945 to 1970.

Chapter 3

Social and Historical Background Post WW1

This chapter discusses briefly the historical and economic factors affecting women in New Zealand from 1918 to the 1970s. How did these elements encourage or discourage the women of the time who wanted to become writers and artists? Were women, given their roles in the home, and the expectations on them to be mothers, wives, and or dutiful daughters, able to find time, space, and financial independence to enable them to write? These points will be dealt with further in the chapters on the novelists and poets.

In New Zealand before the Married Women's Property Act of 1870, designed to protect deserted wives, anything a woman earned or owned was her husband's. Married women up to this time were classed legally as minors together with children and lunatics, originating from the English legal system where, as the jurist Blackstone stated, the 'legal existence of the woman is suspended during marriage'. Sutch notes of married women that under New Zealand law:

> Her chattels became available to her husband and her lands were at his disposal during their joint lives and anything a married woman acquired during her marriage by gift, inheritance, or earnings, went to her husband (Sutch, 1974: 85).

Because New Zealand law was synonymous with British law at this period an interesting aspect of inter-racial marriage occurred. Sutch cites Patricia Grimshaw who records:

> the report in Parliament that in 1881 Māori women, who as women had the right to own land [under tikanga Māori], refused to marry Europeans because, by doing so, they would then become subject to English law (Sutch, 1974: 85).

Despite legal reform, attitudes towards women and finance had not changed all that much by the 1960s. For example, Robyn Du Chateau explains that when her parents separated she went to the lawyer with her mother who told her she would not get anything, that she would have to rely on her husband's compassion. As Du Chateau writes:

> She wasn't allowed to keep anything – the paintings, the furniture, anything at all. Like she walked in and she walked out – she kept her clothes' (Du Chateau in Tolerton, 1997: 60).

Such were the social and legal mores under which many of the writers this book deals with had to live by and work around.

With the social and political upheaval caused by World War One and the worldwide flu epidemic that followed in 1919, the gains of any of the women's organisations towards equality seemed to take a step backwards. Alongside a 'boys back from the war' bias being prominent in employment generally, there were changes in technology that favoured male rather than female employment. For example, there appears to have been a deliberate 'rooting out' or downgrading of women's positions in the New Zealand Public Service throughout the 1920s. Economist Prue Hyman observes:

> All public servants had reduced conditions in this period of intermittent recession, but women were disproportionately downgraded ... [for example]

Women were 16.4 per cent of Post Office employees in 1921, but this had reduced to less than 10 per cent by 1929, with only low-paid, repetitive work available as compared to the higher-skilled postmistress positions filled earlier (Hyman, 1994: 83).

Throughout the 1920s and into the 1930s a concept of 'the family wage' was employed to determine wage rates through the whole economy of New Zealand. Hyman states that:

> The family wage principle had been enunciated by the Arbitration Court, which in 1922 argued that: 'The material requirements of normal life, for the average adult male, includes provision for his family ... In the case of the wage-earner, this right can be effectuated only through wages; therefore the adult male labourer has a right to a family living wage' (quoted in Iverson, 1987). A minimum wage for women was not set by the court until 1937, and then at only 47 per cent of the male rate (Hyman, 1994: 83).

Hyman also notes that the Labour Government, headed by M.J. Savage, during the Depression years of the 1930s continued the policy of the 'family wage' for men as set out in 1922, regardless of whether individual men or women wage earners had dependants. This idea of the man's wage being the norm for families and society became the set concept throughout the period of the 1920s and into the 1930s.

Another international issue that was of concern and contention during the inter-war years was that of married women's nationality. Until the 1920s the legal status of women was that their nationality was deemed to be the same as that of their husbands. An interesting illustration of the absurdity of this policy is the case of Miriam Soljak cited in an essay on women and nationality by Dorothy Page. Page tells of Soljak who married an Austro-Hungarian who had already been in New Zealand for twenty years, but who in 1917 had to register as an 'alien' and as a result his New Zealand born wife Miriam Soljak also had to register as an alien. Page points out that this woman was:

> A New Zealander through and through, she taught before and after her marriage in sole charge Māori schools, spoke Māori fluently, and was concerned for the welfare of the Māori people [indeed, this is far more than could be said for most Pākehā New Zealanders] ... In 1919 [a year after World War One] although (as her daughter put it) she was 'a good Catholic matron expecting her seventh child', she refused point blank to register as an alien; and when at last she was forced to capitulate or go to prison, she insisted that the Tauranga police constable endorse the certificate with the words 'I certify that the applicant has registered under protest' (Page in Brookes, 1986: 165).

During the 1920s and into the 1930s pressure grew among women's groups to have this unfair situation rectified and after the Labour Government was elected in 1935 some progress was made to enable women citizens of New Zealand to differentiate between themselves and their husbands with regard to nationality. The situation was somewhat different in England and other Commonwealth countries. Even after she divorced her husband in the late 1930s Soljak was forced to keep her status as an alien national:

> She travelled to England in 1937 on a British passport marked 'New Zealand born, wife of an alien, now naturalised' and was obliged to report to Scotland Yard every three months ... the New Zealand government was by no means happy with this restriction on its nationality legislation ... At the meeting of

Dominion Prime Ministers [in 1935] and at the 1937 Imperial Conference, it was New Zealand and Australian delegates who set the pace in the discussions on women's nationality ... At the end of the [Second World] war the Commonwealth chose to replace the concept of a single British nationality with that of separate Dominion nationalities embodied in interlocking Nationality Acts ... Thus New Zealand asserted its independence as a nation from Britain, and New Zealand women asserted their independence as citizens from men (Page in Brookes, 1986: 174,175).

These issues carried over into the literary world also. Historian Michael King notes, when discussing art and writing during the decade after World War One, that much of novelist Jane Mander's work was written overseas. King writes:

Those of her books which reached New Zealand were, like the later work of Frances Hodgkins, reviewed with hostility, largely because of what was regarded as 'immoral' content (King, 2004: 320).

Mander's first novel, *The Story of a New Zealand River*, first published in 1920, was set in a Northland timber-milling settlement and focuses on the differences between two generations of women. It challenges the restrictive moral and social code of the main character, Alice Roland, and by contrasting her life with that of her daughter, Asia, explores the possibility of intellectual, sexual and emotional liberation for women. As Rae McGregor wrote:

Mander captures the essence of the New Zealand bush and the speech of New Zealanders. The novel met with good reviews overseas, but some readers in New Zealand perceived in it undertones of immorality, and in the Whāngarei Public Library, for example, the book was put on a discretionary shelf (McGregor, DNZB website, 2007).

Mander was to face persistent criticism in New Zealand for being 'obsessed by sex problems'. While King does not say so, these 'immoral' subjects Mander discusses included venereal disease. However, having 'sex problems' was a common way of dismissing anyone who was 'different' in New Zealand in the early to mid-twentieth century. One feature of the New Zealand of the 1930s was the puritanical attitude to art and literature, and some commentators at the time even associated the economic crisis of the Depression with moral laxity.

In his economic treatise, *The Making of New Zealand*, while discussing the various arguments around the causes of economic collapse in the late 1920s and early 1930s, G.R. Hawke states that:

These arguments, like the even vaguer ones that assert that the economy was 'weak' in the 1920s or that unemployment was present in the 1920s so that the unemployment of a different order of magnitude in the 1930s showed that collapse was inevitable, really owe more to morality than to economics. There were many ideas that just as profligacy in an individual has to be repaid by stringency, so the economy as a whole had to put up with social costs as part of the return to a properly puritan standard of behaviour (Hawke, 1982: 138).

The collapse of the world economic system sparked off by the Wall Street crash in New York's Stock Exchange in 1929 caused many variations in the patterns of women's employment statistics and status. Often women's statistics for employment were excluded from the official data. For example, at the height of the Great Depression, King gives the following figures for New Zealand's jobless as being:

around 80,000 in July 1933. Among these were 20,000 general labourers, 5,000 farm workers and 7,000 building tradesmen. These registrations did not include Māori or women or young men under sixteen (King, 2004: 347).

The Depression of the 1930s and its aftermath tended to downgrade the employment situation of women. This was a state of affairs not rectified significantly by the Labour Government as had been hoped and indeed promised at least until the worst effects of the Depression were over, by 1939 with the outbreak of World War Two, and throughout the war until 1945:

> Women became active in the economy. The percentage in the public service, for example, rose from five percent to 25 per cent in the war years. Women were appointed to the Legislative Council in 1941 and as Justices of the Peace in 1942. Active women were given new status in this period of manpower shortages at home. But the end of the war heralded a headlong rush into marriage (Aitken, 1975: 27).

Social historian Sandra Coney in her history of the Y.W.C.A. quotes Elsie Bennet, General Secretary from 1936 to 1948, who states at the close of World War Two that:

> not enough girls are giving up their jobs to the men they had originally replaced' (Bennet in Coney, 1986: 237).

Coney's response is one of incredulity. She writes of Bennet's proclamation:

> This was an astonishing about-face from the statements during the war about sexual equality being the price of women's war effort, but it was symptomatic of the times. The men had made their sacrifice, now it was the women's turn to surrender their jobs and independence. Marriage and motherhood were asserting themselves in the public mind as women's highest purpose (Coney, 1986: 237).

Social historian Melanie Nolan) discusses the importance of the government in the employment of women. Throughout the twentieth century the State was instrumental in encouraging women to join the work force, particularly during times of labour shortage, as has been seen during the war. This includes both direct employment by the state under good conditions and changes to policies to vary incentives in the economy generally according to the acuteness of the shortage of labour. Nolan states:

> In 1960 the introduction of equal pay in the state sector (a fifth of the female labour force) put them in a privileged position. Thus the state was a major resource for some women, offering them protection and power in training, employment and legislation, as well as in welfare (Nolan, 2000: 36).

Industrialisation in New Zealand 1945-1970
Between 1926 and 1966 participation by women in the general work force grew by nearly seven percent. In 1926 women totalled 20.3% of the estimated workforce. By 1966 this had risen to 27.1%. M. Gilson attributes these figures primarily to the rise of industrialisation. Gilson states:

In New Zealand, as in other economically advanced countries, this meant greater employment opportunities for women in urban centres, while a combination of population growth and rural-urban movement has gradually increased the proportion of women who live in towns and cities where paid employment is available to them (Gilson in Forster, 1969: 187).

Here Gilson concurs with Hawke, who expands the *real politic* of the demographic trends of the period by adding that there was:

> a rising proportion of the population being of working age (15-64) from about 1960, and this trend accelerated in the 1970s. To this added an increased participation rate, that is, more people within the relevant age group wanted a job. A major element in this was the increased tendency of women to seek employment (Hawke, 1982: 333).

Educational advances, particularly among the college educated, have more recently placed more women on a par with men. Hyman backs up the general ideas on the changing patterns of women's employment, post World War Two, but sees the domestic work within relationships as not having changed. She states:

> Technology and social change has led to an increasing range of work being available to women, with domestic work reducing from over one-third of women's jobs to its near disappearance as a live-in occupation during and after the Second World War. Factory, office and professional work of a caring type, at least, became available, although the gender division of labour was as strong as ever (Hyman, 1994: 221).

Earlier Hyman had suggested that increased participation in the labour force along with home labour-saving devices has not decreased women's work at home in their care-giving and nurturing roles. She continues:

> Women in the paid workforce, while spending fewer hours in the home than their counterparts for whom this is a full-time job, still have the longest weeks ... [Schor, 1991] ... Hence the double burden indicates that paid work is not necessarily liberating, especially where it is a financial necessity (Hyman, 1994: 220).

In her 1990 publication *A Woman's Wage* U.S. feminist economist, Alice Kessler-Harris addresses issues that demonstrate the ways in which the changing historical meaning of the wage relation is constructed by society's conceptions of gender. It is too simple to assert that both men's and women's wages are set entirely by supply and demand for different types of labour in the market place. She focuses on three sets of issues that capture the transformation of women's roles: the battle over the minimum wage for women, which exposes the relationship between family ideology and workplace demands; the argument over equal pay for equal work, which challenges gendered patterns of self-esteem and social organization; and the debate over comparable worth, which seeks to incorporate traditionally female values into new work and family trajectories. On the meaning of 'wages' Kessler-Harris states:

> If the wage is, as most economists readily acknowledge, simultaneously a set of ideas about how people can and should live and a marker of social status, then it contains within it a set of social messages and a system of meanings that influence the way women and men behave (Kessler-Harris, 1990: 7).

In other words, while equal wages in the dollar sense may mean the same thing to men and women employees in any given industry, the male/female relationship within that context may still be unequal due to the balance of 'family ideology and workplace demands' alluded to by Hyman.

The question in relation to this my study is: how did these macro-economic and macro-social events and movements affect individual women living within the society of New Zealand who wanted to become writers and artists? How did social mores and expectations on women, particularly from the end of the Second World War up until the 1970s, impinge on the ambitions and aspirations of women who felt, perhaps, that their own 'artistic vision', in the broadest sense of the concept, was stymied by family obligations and economic dependency. Jock Phillips suggests veterans returning from the war wanted to 'settle down in comfortable domestic life', and that 'antagonism between the sexes' was a post-WW2 characteristic of New Zealand society. Leslie Hall suggests that married women during this period were often forced to play 'the deferential little-woman role' in unhappy marriages.

In Chapter 7 I discuss these elements in relation to three specific examples of 'writers/artists' marriages and the dynamics of the male and female partners within them plus one example of a woman writer who was a solo parent at the time when there was no Domestic Purposes Benefit and society frowned upon single women who wanted to keep their children. Butterworth's example is significant because it documents her attempts to become a writer whilst struggling with the restrictions on women. The social and economic circumstances of the post WW2 period, from the evidence above, meant that women's lives were framed and restricted by boundaries that did not generally regard them as equal participants in society.

For the women writers of the period, their economic choices made balancing a life between creative writing and the expected women's role of the period very difficult. This was exacerbated by the often misogynist attitudes of the men returning from war service, whose experiences had often damaged and traumatised them to a degree that they rejected women for not having participated in those experiences, and thus being unable to write on topics they considered relevant and important. This is discussed in the following chapter on the literary background. As a poem by 'Alien' called 'Without Malice' puts it:

You, being a modern poet
Must write real he-man stuff
So you will take slabs of prose
And cuts it into chunks like this;
There need be no rhyme nor reason in it ...

No top-notch New Zealand poet any longer
Writes ballads like Jessie Mackay
Or bird-songs like Eileen Duggan
Or lyricisms like Helena Henderson
Or tree-poems like Nellie Macleod ...

And anyway they're only women
(Alien, 2004: 179-180).

Chapter 4

Literary Background

Much writing of history, in the conventional writing of human endeavour, has been just that: 'his story'. There have been significant attempts to redress this situation in the recent past by feminist writers and academics, such as Aorewa McLeod, Adrienne Rich, and Sarah Ell. However, much of the documentation of human life has been from the male perspective. This chapter on the literary background of New Zealand writing discusses these matters in relation to the women writers during the period the present study covers. Ell writes in the introduction to her second volume of two books on pioneer women in New Zealand:

> History books can tell us what happened, and to whom, but only first hand accounts can tell us how it *felt*, to those directly involved or on the outside looking in. And much of women's history is undocumented – few history textbooks record the privations of confinement, or the desolation of the loss of a loved one, or the domestic reality of life on the frontier (Ell, 1993: 9).

As I argue later when discussing Curnow's following of T.S. Eliot's 'ban on the personal', a fundamental difference between men's and women's writing is expressed in this period of New Zealand literature.

Georgians versus Modernists

In New Zealand between 1945 and 1970 the literary, academic and gender politics were entangled in the controversy between Georgian and Modernist literary styles. Poet James Reeves states in his introduction to the anthology *Georgian Poetry*:

> The word 'Georgian', as applied to a body of poetry written in English during the second and third decades of the twentieth century, came into use purely as a descriptive term. By the end of that period it had become a term of critical abuse, and by the beginning of the Second World War it was merely an archaism (Reeves, 1962: xi).

This reflected an international literary debate. For example, the W.G. Bebbington compilation *Introducing Modern Poetry: An Anthology*, published by Eliot's publishers for whom he worked included just one woman, Edith Sitwell, out of the 21 poets selected. This anthology was first published in 1944, a year before Allen Curnow's collection in 1945 which had only 2 women represented among the 16 poets included. While Bebbington's anthology may not have directly influenced Curnow's inclusion choices, it almost certainly indicates a trend in the poetic politics of the English speaking world of the post-war period.

In 1930 in the poetry collection, *Kowhai Gold: An Anthology of Contemporary New Zealand Verse*, edited by Quentin Pope, a line was drawn between the Georgian poetry identity in New Zealand and the mainly 'manly' Modernist manifestation of verse writing that came to prominence in the 1930s and late 1940s and in some form continued through to the post-modern era of the late 1980s. *The Oxford Companion to New Zealand Literature* says that Curnow, in his 1945 introduction to his anthology reflecting on *Kowhai Gold*: 'argues gently that there was little justification for publishing so much that is "trivial if sincere" because the "body of New Zealand verse is not to be enlarged by seeking numbers of additional names"'.

However, it also appears specific to the post-war culture of New Zealand literature that in many respects the New Zealand 'Modernists' also became actively anti-women to some degree. The Modernists equated Georgian poetry with 'femininity', and therefore deemed it flowery and inferior. 1945 was a watershed year in regard to the influence of the so-called new thinking in New Zealand literature. The publication of Curnow's anthology, *A Book of New Zealand Verse*, in that year continued what was the mid-1930s undermining of the 'Georgian' school of poetry, and therefore the 'female' tradition, in New Zealand poetry which had been strong up to that point.

This was not always so. In fact, the original English Georgians were very much a male oriented group of writers. In the Penguin Poets series on Georgian poets only one, Victoria Sackville-West, of the nineteen poets represented was a woman. And no-one would consider the likes of Wilfred Owen, Robert Graves, Rupert Brooke or Siegfried Sassoon as writing in a style imbued with 'femininity', or that was in any way 'flowery and inferior'. In his introduction to the Penguin anthology, James Reeves spells out what he thinks defines the movement by stating that Georgianism essentially was the:

> celebration of England ... the English countryside, English crafts ... poems about country cottages, old furniture, moss-covered barns, rose-scented lanes, apple and cherry orchards ... and the threat to country life which educated readers feared from the growth of urbanism (Reeves, 1962: xv).

While it might appear that the New Zealand Georgians were simply copying the English Georgians a decade or two later it is important to remember that up until the 1940s New Zealand was still very much a rural society and much of the poets' inspiration at the time came from the natural beauty and uniqueness of the New Zealand landscape and bush, to which the name *Kowhai Gold* attests.

By the 1960s Curnow's position in relation to the *Kowhai Gold* anthology generation had hardened further. In the introduction to the 1966 edition of *The Penguin Book of New Zealand Verse* Curnow, as the editor, states that Pope's anthology 'could only corrupt the better, as it encouraged the worse'. He described it as a 'lamentable anthology' ... that 'preserved twenty-three names from the earlier selections of Alexander and Currie,[1] and added thirty-five new ones, of whom eighteen were women'. Why did Curnow add that seemingly unnecessary adjunct to the last sentence 'of whom eighteen were women'? He seems to imply that too many women poets are being published who have no real talent. Curnow also states that 'Hobbyists and ungifted amateurs crowded Marris's annual *New Zealand Best Poems* during the thirties'. If a comparison is made between pre-1945 anthologies of New Zealand poetry several trends relating to gender balance emerge.

For example, if we look at a number of the Marris *New Zealand Best Poems* series there are significantly more women poets being published throughout the 1930s and into the 1940s than men. One point of interest here is that despite his later disparaging remarks about Marris's *New Zealand Best Poems* books, a sonnet by Denis Glover appears in the 1934 edition. But it was 1934 that also saw Glover and fellow editor, Ian Milner, present the first openly anti-Georgian anthology, *New Poems*. In the foreword the editors state their intentions of moving away from poetry that was of the Georgian tradition, which they saw as:

> sentimental rhapsodising over love, flowers or sunsets seems to pass as poetry. A predilection for decorative lyricising and emotional embroidery, weakly reminiscent of pre-war Georgian verse, has produced in this country a lifeless growth which, though not necessarily insincere, is in no sense creative (Glover & Milner, 1934: foreword).

---

[1] Editors of the 1926 anthology *A Treasury of New Zealand Verse*.

It is not too big a step from this beginning to the derogatory terminology used by Curnow ten years later. Words like 'decorative', 'embroidery', 'weakly' all act as a catalyst to the masculinist putting down of women writers prevalent in the post-WW2 era. And another telling and prophetic aspect of the New Poems publication is, that of the ten poets represented, only one is a woman, Jean Alison. By contrast, if we look at Marris's yearly anthologies New Zealand Best Poems showing men and women's entry numbers for selected years:

Year	Men	Women
1933	8	10
1934	9	9
1936	9	9
1937	7	12
1938	6	11
1941	6	8
Total for period	45	59

Also, compare the above figures with the 1937 volume Verse Alive: number two. This book was also a new venture by those male writers who would go on to dominate much of the literary trends and taste throughout the period which this study covers. Of the eleven poets featured in Verse Alive: number two there is only one woman, Robin Hyde. The joint editorship is by H. Winston Rhodes and Denis Glover, who, as has been noted, only three years earlier was published in Marris's New Zealand Best Poems. In their foreword the editors of Verse Alive state:

> There is some reason for saying that poetry is being killed by kindness, by an artificial and academic respect which raises it beyond the level to which the average man cares to go. He believes that he has no appreciation of poetical imagery or rhythmical speech, and turns to the sporting column which is packed full of wildly grotesque images, or talks to his neighbour in colloquial phrases which often contain the very rhythms that the contemporary poet uses (Rhodes and Glover, 1937: 5).

The editors' comments can be interpreted as setting a blueprint for the philosophy developing which would dominate literary into the post-war period. The fact that this publication has one of the first poems to be aired publicly by the young Allen Curnow is significant as this is the beginning of what would become the male domination of literary 'politically correct' ideals and ideas, based on a poetic framework of the 'average man' who would rather 'turn to the sporting column' than read the poetry of an 'artificial and academic' form of expression. There seems to be no place in this 'radical' Weltanschauung for the woman poet, or indeed the woman who talks to her neighbour over the back fence 'in colloquial phrases' either.

Binarism is an academic term that is used to understand and define opposite and often opposing points of view. It is essentially a mode of thought predicated on stable oppositions such as good and evil or male and female and is seen as a specific dichotomy subscribed to or reinforced in such thought. In relation to the present work it could be said that a binary mindset was set up by the Modernist male writers to set themselves apart from the Georgian females. As Lawrence Jones states of the Modernist men in his essay on 'Mulgan, Marris, Schroder' published in A Book in the Hand, they: 'defined themselves by opposition, whether to an idea or a literary movement, such as Georgianism'. Thus, it is the Modernists who set up a binary predisposition in relation to the male-female literary conceits of the period.

There were, of course, male poets who were considered Georgian. One example was the poet, publisher and printer, Bob Gormack, who according to Noel Waite writing in Chapter Twelve of *A Book in the Hand*, felt compelled:

> to mount something of a rearguard action in support of the much-maligned 'Georgian' poets. In the introductory remarks, 'The ballad of Kaka Thompson' was cited as an example of 19th-century ballad-making that provided 'a most satisfactory answer to the many contemporary New Zealand writers — particularly those of the modern Caxton Press school — who still maintain, either directly or by provocative innuendo, that their native land has no poetical and literary traditions worth following or worth investigating' (Waite, 2000: 191).

In Gormack we find something of interest in the topsy-turvey nature of the Georgian-Modernist debate in New Zealand literature. It would appear ironic that the Modernists who were credited with giving our literature its first true expression of our 'New Zealandness' are seen as believing that 'their native land has no poetical and literary traditions worth following or worth investigating' Canterbury academic, Patrick Evans, investigates this conundrum and writes:

> The Phoenix generation ... particularly .... Identified with Middleton Murray, who had made the beginnings of his reputation with his savaging of the fourth Georgian anthology [in England] of 1919. By identifying with him the young New Zealand poets [of the 1930s] automatically assumed an opposition to the Georgian strain in New Zealand poetry ... this was to become complicated because it opposed something many of them had within themselves (Evans, 1990: 76-77).

While in his 1981 book, *In the Glass Case*, poet and critic C.K. Stead quotes Alistair Te Ariki Campbell who said that R.A.K. Mason [that is, a major male poet] 'is undoubtedly a Georgian poet' (Campbell in Stead, 1981: 182) and Stead discusses the fact that there are 'good Georgians and bad Georgians ... Georgian realists and Georgian sentimentalists'. Although he refers to 'the best of the Georgians' Stead still comes down on the negative side of the Georgian-Modernist debate, as do the majority of the critics of the era, from Curnow to Baxter to Glover. This would not appear so bad if it were just a matter of literary taste, for example. However, the fact that 'Georgianism' became a derogatory term analogous with 'female' in the literary/poetry world of the 1930s and into the following decades denotes an underlying trend towards anti-female behaviour of male writers, publishers and critics in the period this study covers.

No place for a woman

English language convention often uses the words 'man' and 'men' to denote all people, men and women. At least in the grammatical convention of 'man' meaning a 'person' it is assumed that the term implies women also. However, in the extreme 'masculinist' tradition developing in the literary world of New Zealand in this period women almost ceased to exist, linguistically at least. It is interesting to note here that this phenomenon reaches far beyond just the New Zealand situation. For example, American poet Louise Bernikow notes that the 'heightened states of emotion out of which male poets were creating poetry were praised as revolutionary: the heightened states of female emotion were denigrated and dismissed as second-rate'.

Although Bernikow is considering 19th Century English poetry the underlying truth is the same in the middle 20th Century New Zealand literary scene with regard

23

to women and men writers. Even Robin Hyde, who appears in both of Curnow's anthologies, Caxton and Penguin, and is the only woman poet in *Verse Alive: number two*, does not escape the scathing male put-downs. For example, Curnow's remarks about her as a poet. Having more or less pitied her for her emotional instability he then states how Hyde 'fought to free her vision from its literary swathings – and in verse her worst enemy was the passionate crush on poetry with which she began. Her writing was near hysteria, more often than not, and she was incurably exhibitionistic'. Here Curnow exhibits the attitudes I have identified. He constructs for New Zealand readers a view of a stereotypical 'female poet' alluded to by Bernikow.

American feminist critic Joanna Russ considers the problems inherent in the negative attitudes towards writing by women and why it is often not taken seriously by the literary establishment. The cover has a series of statements that typify some of the sexist thinking on writing by women authors, whether they are novelists, poets, or non-fiction writers. The parts quoted in capital letters are in red on the original cover:

> SHE DIDN'T WRITE IT. But it's clear she did the deed ... SHE WROTE IT, BUT SHE SHOULDN'T HAVE. It's political, sexual, masculine, feminist ... SHE WROTE IT, BUT LOOK WHAT SHE WROTE ABOUT. The bedroom, the kitchen, her family. Other women! ... SHE WROTE IT, BUT SHE ONLY WROTE ONE OF IT. 'Jane Eyre. Poor dear, that's all she ever' ... SHE WROTE IT, BUT SHE ISN'T REALLY AN ARTIST, AND IT ISN'T REALLY ART. It's a thriller, a romance, a children's book. It's sci fi! ... SHE WROTE IT, BUT SHE HAD HELP. Robert Browning. Branwell Brontë. Her own 'masculine side' ... SHE WROTE IT, BUT SHE'S AN ANOMALY. Woolf. With Leonard's help ... SHE WROTE IT, BUT ...' (Russ, 1984).

The implications of this for the women writers in New Zealand are clear, particularly during the post-war period up to the 1970s. Russ, in a chapter titled 'Anomalousness', quotes Dolores Palomo on how the 'refined eyes of scholarship condemn 'one half to two thirds of the fiction penned in the eighteenth century' as minor, mediocre, or salacious – that is, the fiction written by women'. With what we know of the women writers in New Zealand, beginning in the 1930s, this demonstrates how these women writers seemed to take on a lower status, not only as writers but also as human beings. Russ quotes American poet Erica Jong describing her literary education:

> being a woman means, unfortunately, believing a lot of male definitions ... I learned what an orgasm was from D.H. Lawrence, disguised as Lady Chatterley ... (For years I measured my orgasms against Lady Chatterley's and wondered what was wrong with me ...) I learned from Dostoevski that they (women) have no religious feeling. I learned from Swift and Pope that they have too much religious feeling (and therefore can never be quite rational). I learned from Faulkner that they are earth-mothers and at one with the moon and the tide and the crops. I learned from Freud that they have deficient superegos and are forever 'incomplete' (Jong in Russ, 1984: 89).

Jong continues, stating a view that is particularly pertinent concerning the attitude of the New Zealand male writers to women writers of the period. She explains that poetry for her was masculine. A visiting male writer to her university:

> went on and on about how women *couldn't possibly* be authors. Their experience was too limited ... They didn't know blood and guts and fucking

whores and puking in the streets ... this [she said] made me miserable (Jong: in Russ, 1984: 89-90).

The latter certainly reflects what some of the male writers in New Zealand thought and felt about women writers and their literary endeavours. However, upon consideration, it shows up the men. For example, the fact that women menstruate and some experience childbirth which can often be painful may be said to negate the argument that women do not experience blood and physical extremes. It could be said that until you experience giving birth you don't know about 'blood and guts'.

The underlying sense of violence as 'male expression' as reported by Jong, as being the only legitimate poetic form, also comes into play in the literary world of New Zealand. After describing a particularly nasty scene of rape performed by a New Zealand soldier in a novel set during WW2, as an act of revenge on a nurse who dared to criticise a failed military action, Kai Jensen in *Whole Men* continues by writing that war literature was an extreme manifestation of the misogynist way that women were often depicted in our poetry and fiction. In a 1968 essay on the state of New Zealand poetry, Curnow's conclusion summed up his views with a quotation from his poem:

Love-poems if you like. But keep them short.
It's all *vieux jeu*, unless you're crude and stark.
She won't, we needn't, read them. Sport,
Tell her you love her, and tell her in the dark
(Curnow, 1987: 229).

The audience is male
The poet is imagined here as male, as is the audience of Curnow's paper, while the beloved is presumed to be uninterested in poetry. Jensen discusses Fairburn's misogynist masterpiece, *The Woman Problem*. In this long essay, which Jensen describes as being 'semi-serious', the poet A.R.D. Fairburn argues for male domination of women in marriage, on the grounds that equality between men and women was a 'sentimental' and 'romantic' heresy, spread by feminists and homosexuals. Women were happier in marriage where husbands kept a firm hand on the reins. This was better for society as well, since Fairburn claimed that women were inherently immoral and anti-social because of their natural focus on children and family:

most women have little notion of abstract justice ... they are incapable of attaching importance to principles of any kind ... women's minds are not designed for the purpose of making judgements on matters that call for objective consideration. [Women who had] acquired certain masculine habits of mind, through their association with intelligent men [might be] most charming [but were] usually marginal creatures in the book of Genesis (Fairburn, 1967, 18-19).

Imagine how much deeper would have been Jong's despair had she been a New Zealand woman writer reading these words in 1967, when *The Woman Problem* was first published. Fairburn discusses the development of civilization as the work of men, whereas the work of women he sees as coming from natural instincts, therefore something for men to tame. He states that civilization implies the repression of natural desires and that:

The higher refinements of civilization are the work of man, not of woman. His strongest motive has been, at all times, the finding of creative satisfaction.

Woman receives this satisfaction as her birthright. Man, being all but irrelevant to the business of procreation, has had to invent other means of satisfying his creative instinct (Fairburn, 1967: 34).

Fairburn then goes on to quote the French novelist Baudelaire who said: 'Woman is natural, therefore abominable'. He may have meant that woman is completely tied up with the biological process, and has no real sympathy for the world of art-for-art's-sake which had, in his time, begun to detach itself consciously from the full context of life – just as the homosexual is detached from society.

> But we may suspect that Baudelaire, being a man of subtle mind, meant a good deal more than that. He was, perhaps, not merely justifying the unreal world of 'pure aesthetics' and 'pure sex', but asserting also, for those with ears keen enough to hear, that woman presents a constant threat to civilized life (Fairburn, 1967: 35).

While Fairburn may be expressing extreme views to get across a less extreme or even satirical point, it appeared that these views were common currency among male intellectuals during the 1940s, 1950s and 1960s, in New Zealand and elsewhere in the Western World. This helps to build a picture of the underlying misogynist nature of their attitude to women writers. The implication that women are somehow indifferent to the finer feelings, as expressed in Curnow's quote from Glover's poem, for example, means that women have no ideas beyond their natural instincts. Like nature itself, this indifference extends into their personal relationships. The poet, James K. Baxter, in an unpublished letter to fellow poet, Victor O'Leary, states:

> Women are cruel. I think you are sometimes too nice to them – but perhaps you try harder than I have done' (Baxter, unpublished poem: c1950s).[2]

Ban on the personal
However, if we turn from the question of women being 'natural' and men being somehow supernatural or even supra-natural, and look at the reality of the women's lives, which often consisted of decades of domestic drudgery, then we can appreciate why women were not at the forefront of the intellectual or cultural aspects of society. Carolyn Heilbrun considers these issues and shows through the lives of individual writers how erroneous some male assumptions were in relation to their ideas of the male/female utopias. She quotes Rich's discussion of the human condition. Rich notes: 'those who speak largely of the human condition are usually those most exempt from its oppressions – whether of sex, race, or servitude'.

Heilbrun goes on to discuss autobiography in women's writing, stating that while it had become common for both women and men, that 'it was chiefly in Rich's generation of women poets – Plath, Sexton, Kumin, Kizer, Cooper, Levertov – that T.S. Eliot's ban upon the personal was defied'. It is here that the women poets of New Zealand from the 1940s to the 1970s were also denigrated, for Curnow in particular was an advocate for the Eliot version of Modernist poetic expression, in which the 'personal' was not acceptable.

The battle that women had between their social, or as Fairburn believed, their 'natural' position in the world, whereby they have no need for creative or artistic

---

[2] From a copy of a letter given to me by Victor O'Leary, who was a member of the Glenco group of Wellington Poets in the 1950s, which also included Baxter. The letter is headed 'School Publications, Dept. of Education, Wellington, 9th August 1962'. Baxter's letter was accompanied by a poem dedicated to 'Vic O'Leary' – the title of the poem is 'Mazeppa'.

expression, comes under scrutiny when Heilburn discusses the writing of, among others, American poet, Anne Sexton. Sexton had explained to an interviewer:

> Until I was twenty-eight I had a kind of buried self who didn't know she could do anything but make white sauce and diaper babies ... I was trying my damndest to lead a conventional life, for that was how I was brought up, and it was what my husband wanted of me. But one can't build little white picket fences to keep nightmares out ... (Sexton in Heilbrun, 1988: 70).

The importance of this passage, Heilbrun argues, lies in its truth that women could not previously express. She explains:

> there are two other points that Diane Middlebrook has clearly identified for us: that 'Sexton experienced the home as a sphere of confinement and stultification,' and that she escaped through the way of death. For Sexton and Plath, suicide became part of life, so violent was the action necessary for rebirth and truth (Heilbrun, 1988: 70).

Heilbrun quotes Carolyn Kizer's words which seem to sum up the plight of women poets down through the ages:

> From Sappho to myself, consider the fate of women
> How unwomanly to discuss it!
> (Kizer in Heilbrun, 1988: 70).

These issues of women's creativity can be seen in the work of New Zealand novelist and poet Robin Hyde, who like Plath, Sexton and Woolf, committed suicide in what could be regarded as an act of creative destruction. In his introduction to *The Penguin Book of New Zealand Verse* Curnow again shows his own predilection towards Eliot's 'ban upon the personal' poetical philosophy. He respects Hyde enough as a poet to include her in this anthology, although, as in his earlier Caxton anthology, he remains critical of her use of personal motifs. While he states that in the last five years of her life she produced her best work he goes on to comment that:

> By incessant writing, incessant change, she fought to free her vision from its literary swathings – and in verse her worst enemy was the passionate crush on poetry with which she began. Her writing was near hysteria, more often than not, and she was incurably exhibitionistic: any moment we are likely to get the awful archness of her lines on 'Katherine Mansfield': (Curnow, 1966: 57).

He was referring to Hyde's sympathetic lines on Mansfield:

> Our little Darkness, in the shadow sleeping,
> Among the strangers you could better trust
> Right was your faring, Wings: ...
> (Hyde in Curnow, 1966: 57).

Giving New Zealand women 'a swelled head'
Curnow says of Hyde that New Zealand had concentrated all its forces to confound one who had neither the will nor the opportunity to escape early, like Katherine Mansfield. Curnow quotes from an unpublished letter by eccentric New Zealand poet and pretender to the Polish throne, Count Geoffrey Potocki de Montalk, to the

poet A.R.D. Fairburn, stating his view that: 'K.M. has had one most deplorable result – that of giving N.Z. women a swelled head'. This is interesting as in his memoir de Montalk writes of poet V. Alison Grant, one of the *Kowhai Gold* poets, as being:

> One of the most remarkable of the authors and artists of New Zealand in my generation ... She is an unusually gifted person, but when young was fantastically ill-mannered in the best New Zealand fashion ... She used to be a serious reminder of why one had left New Zealand. And also of the fact that choice New Zealanders are much more gifted than their opposite numbers in England (de Montalk, 1983: 30-31).

Here, it seems he may 'give women a swelled head'. De Montalk touches on the New Zealander abroad in his comments on Grant, something I explore further in the chapter on women novelists. Curnow's approach towards poetry, his belief that it should not be personal but somehow objective, puts him squarely on the masculinist side of the division, with his ideas reflecting an essentialist idea of maleness as superior in poetic expression. Hyman discusses this type of dichotomy, stating:

> Orthodox economics is based on the positivist approach of the natural sciences. Feminist critiques of science see this approach as imbued with erroneous notions of value neutrality, objectivity and dualistic thinking. Dualisms such as mind/body, abstract/concrete, objective/subjective, rational/emotional and, by inference at least, male/female, with the first involving a superior level of thinking, are criticised as limited, hierarchical and gender based. The separation of knower from known, with detachment a major virtue, means that scientific measurement alone can contribute to knowledge, with no supplementation from experience or from sensual, spiritual or emotional knowledge (Hyman, 1994: 35).

While Hyman is discussing economics and its social value, this can be applied to suggest there are similar biases in male poets' thinking during the post-war period on poetry and intellectual life generally in relation to their art, with their ban upon the personal and their attitudes towards women, and women writers in particular. It is with this background of thought in mind that the period 1945 to 1970 became a cultural 'wasteland' for the women writers of the period. Poet Alan Brunton sums up the situation regarding the place of women in the poetic scheme of things with reference to the male poets. In *Years Ago Today* he writes:

> The 'poet', as defined by increasingly surly anthologies, wavered between victim and victor but was in any case authoritarian, and patriarchal. The hero was a man under an existential curse, whose fate was to be outnumbered and caught in a hopeless situation and destroyed: he was the female's necessary sacrifice. The vision was monarchical, solar and defensive. The female was regarded as either dully domestic or sexually hysterical, or both. The ethical basis of this myth was where it was most convoluted. Sacrifice of the self is necessary but sacrifice increases pollution. This should not cause pessimism for only in pollution can redemption be sought. The cruel twist is that pollution is the absence of god. Curnow's god was absent and therefore he despaired (Brunton, 1997: 36).

This male adherence to the 'non-feeling', non-personal usurping of the literary world, when academic objectivity has been made 'the law' of literary taste, appears to have begun in the 1930s and followed through from the post-war period to the 1970s. Academic Anne Else writes that those:

working beyond such circles, including most women writers, became increasingly marginalized from the body of work emerging as New Zealand literature. The records of the women writers' organisations suggest that from the 1940s to the late 1960s, the majority of members thought of 'New Zealand literature' as something being written elsewhere, principally by men – some of whom they invited to lecture to them – rather than something they themselves could take part in producing (Else, 1993: 451).

However, this too began to change. In relation to the male 'establishment' of writers and publishers I have written elsewhere:

But, however much the 'radicals' of the '30s still saw themselves in that vein, they had become by the end of the 1960s the literary 'establishment' of New Zealand. The fact that, except for Janet Paul, the main publishers of the time were male, Pākehā, and becoming increasingly conservative in relation to the '60s generation now growing up around them, meant they were beginning to lose their relevance (O'Leary, 2007: 19).

In her editorial to the 'women's' issue of Landfall Linda Hardy discussed the then current prestige and popularity of 'women's writing', and asked the question:

What need is there, then, for Landfall to put out a 'special issue' devoted to 'women's writing'? A rough count in five recent issues of this magazine gives me a total of 29 women contributing stories and poems, as against 39 men; far from equality, but not 'silence' either (Hardy, 1985: 400).

A similar analysis of an earlier five issues of Landfall 1951 to 1952 reveals that there were 10 women alongside 34 men, with one of the women, Ruth France, using the male pseudonym, Paul Henderson. Another analysis of a further five issues from late 1952 to 1954 reveals an even more dramatic picture when there were 36 men writers as against 2 women writers. In 1955 and 1956 there were 28 men and 6 women. And during the so-called liberal 1960s, the years 1968 to 1969, the gap increased rather than decreased, with 49 men published in five issues, and only 9 women.

These figures illustrate a central feature of thisstudy, that is, the exclusion or limiting of women writers during the period 1945-70. However, two recent issues of Landfall in 1999 show a change. In those issues the total of 28 men and 19 women indicates a seismic shift. This, like the demand for equal pay, suggests that there has been some movement towards equality from the period of the late 1940s to more recent times in relation to a more equitable distribution of capital, both financial and intellectual, between men and women.

This is seen in the workings of the New Zealand Women Writers' Society, a group of women based in Wellington, which began in 1932 and finished in 1991. For example, the Wellington poet, novelist and journalist, Pat Lawlor, is eulogised in the 1982 history of the society:

Mr Lawlor chaired the first meeting of the Society convened by Nellie Donovan and until his death at the age of 86 in 1979, he kept up his interest and encouragement and was affectionately known as 'the father of the Society'. On the Society's 25th Birthday he presented a collection of Katherine Mansfield books and manuscripts (France et al, 1982: 5).

This was a prize for a competition for writing about Wellington. Lawlor was in 1977 the only male and was elected Hon. Vice-President of the Society. Another example of the Women Writers of New Zealand Society seeking male approval can be seen in the 1953 publication *POEMS: Anthology of New Zealand Women Writers*. In some respects, it may be seen as an answer to the arrogance and negativity displayed in Curnow's attitude to women poets via his rejection of Georgianism and their lack of representation in his 1945 *A Book of New Zealand Verse*.

However, the editorial for *POEMS: Anthology of New Zealand Women Writers* was written by a man, Alan R. Dunlop. The opposite situation to Lawlor and Dunlop's 'patronage' can be seen in women like Elizabeth Pudsey Dawson, better known as Peter Dawson in New Zealand literary circles, who was a loyal and generous friend to both Sargeson and Frame. Described as 'left-wing and lesbian' Dawson's assistance to many other writers, the majority of whom were men, over a forty-year period in New Zealand from the late 1940s until she died in 1986, could be seen as an attempt to buy acceptance in the literary scene. The fact that many who benefited from her generosity never acknowledged her support makes it surprising that she did not do more to assist women writers of the period other than Frame.

Chapter 5

Women Poets

This chapter centres on the poets of the period covered by this study. In the context of the status of women's poetry written and published during the time of the post-war period up to the 1970s there is evidence to suggest that male publishers and male poets in particular were quite disparaging towards women poets. Many negative attitudes towards women poets came from a particular aspect of male writing, from those writers trying to build a New Zealand literature based on a philosophy of the 'man alone' ethos, underpinned by male war experience.

This would later be epitomized by the National Party's Prime Minister of the 1970s and 1980s, Robert Muldoon, as the 'ordinary bloke', although I doubt that poets such as Allen Curnow, James K. Baxter or Denis Glover would appreciate this association. Academic Mark Williams points out that Blanche Baughan and Ursula Bethell, as with many other women writers of the period, have been caught up in the ongoing disputes about the Modernist philosophy of the 1930s and its effects on earlier generations of writers. A.R.D. Fairburn, R.A.K. Mason and Glover were all central movers of that movement, as was Curnow.

In 2009 I attended the funeral of Alistair Te Ariki Campbell at Pukerua Bay north of Wellington where he had lived with his second wife, poet Meg Campbell, for many years. At the funeral a poem by Campbell's first wife Fleur Adcock, now a major British poet, was read by her sister, novelist and poet Marilyn Duckworth. This poem made a telling point:

> of his romantic looks
> and silly girls like me,
> foolish enough to marry
> what I wanted to be
> (Adcock, 2009: 13).

This elicited some laughter from those who knew the two, and it was a witty comment on their relationship. However, Adcock had previously written:

> I write when and wherever I can (not always easy); and my commitment to poetry is total' (Adcock in Ensing, 1977: 15).

a good example of how women writers struggled to become recognised as poets in their own right.

Ruth Gilbert

The poet Ruth Gilbert provides another example of the experience of women poets during the period this study covers, her first publication appearing in 1941. Gilbert offers a case study for these women poets, as she is at the heart of the controversy regarding the antagonism that some men writers and publishers displayed towards the work of their women counterparts up to the feminist movement of the 1970s.

Evidence of this antipathy can be found in 1957 when the literary magazine *numbers* 7 published a letter by fellow poet Willow Macky in which she criticises the critics of the New Zealand literary scene, in particular the editor of the *numbers* series, poet Louis Johnson, for his unfavourable review of the latest book by Gilbert, *The Sunlit Hour*. Macky's letter becomes both a plea to her male colleagues and an indictment against them when it comes to their treatment of their female counterparts. She states:

> Most women, if they wish for success, will try to conform, monkey-like, to the masculine pattern; others, by remaining true to their feminine insight, risk opposition and failure in male-dominated fields (Macky in *numbers* 7, 1957: 26).

The question is: why was this the case? This letter is evidence that women actually felt like this and expressed these frustrations about the way they were treated by male editors.

The 1970 cut-off point for this study roughly coincides with the emergence of 'second wave' feminist movement in New Zealand. However, when lesbian-feminist poet Heather McPherson was asked about her early attempts to get into print before and around 1970 she said she had poems published in *Landfall* and had approached Leo Bensemann, then Caxton Press and *Landfall* editor, with a collection of poems, mentioning to him that she had become a feminist. His reply was that Rita Cook (Rita Angus) had become a feminist 'but it didn't do her any good either'.

These examples illustrate some of the difficulties and antipathies existing between the men and women literary figures during the period of my study. They illustrate some of the restraints and difficulties women writers worked under. Gilbert's experience reflects the hurt and feeling of unfair treatment given to women writers by their male counterparts, editors and publishers. As early as 1943 her poem 'Shooting Season', unpublished until the 1988 collection *Early Poems: 1938-1944*, describes male writers taking pot-shots at female writers, just two years after her first appearance in print.

When man goes forth
At rise of sun
With haversack
And well-greased gun

How most unpleasant
To be a pheasant;
And what abysmal luck
To find oneself a duck
(Gilbert, 1988: 38).

Nielsen Wright's book on her quotes Gilbert stating that 'Shooting Season' was written in 1943. However, when Wright interviewed Gilbert in 1988 she associated 'Shooting Season' with James K. Baxter and Louis Johnson as the shooters. Wright found this impossible since the poem was dated 1943. He continues that he knew Gilbert felt she was under attack from Baxter and Johnson in the 1950's and 1960's, as had Eileen Duggan at PEN committee meetings.

A brief profile of Gilbert's life and publishing history illustrates her place in both literary and social settings during the period. Born in 1917 at Greytown, Wairarapa, as an adult she could be regarded as typical of many New Zealand women during and after WW2, as she married and had children. During her long literary career Gilbert's poems have appeared in newspapers, books and magazines. Her poems were published in C.A. Marris's *New Zealand's Best Poems*, *Art in New Zealand*, *The Evening Post*, *Lyric Poems of New Zealand*, Johnson's *New Zealand Poetry Yearbook*, and Frank McKay's *Poetry New Zealand*. She has also been published in Australia, Canada, England, Ireland, and her work has been broadcast on the BBC and the former NZBC (now Radio New Zealand). Her publishing and writing career provides perspective on the literary trends and views of other authors in relation to the gender politics of the period.

Gilbert's post-war poems to 1950 show how her career as a published poet began, also how it was undermined by what I argue were the misogynist views prevalent among publishers and anthologists of the time. Brasch included Gilbert in the literary magazine *Landfall* only once:[3] *Landfall 11*, March 1948. 'Lazarus' sequence: 1 Betrothed to Lazarus; 2 The Sisters of Lazarus; 3 Lazarus speaks, which were subsequently published by Reed in 1949 under the title *Lazarus and Other Poems*. The author note for the *Landfall* issue states that her work had also appeared in *Art in New Zealand, The Evening Post* and *New Zealand Best Poems*.

For Gilbert, 1948 was a very successful year. Her work 'Overheard in a garden: Anthem poems' was published in *Yearbook of the Arts in New Zealand*. She was also published by *Quill*, the magazine of the Society of New Zealand Women Writers and Artists. A note in *Quill* about 'Lazarus' states the poem won the Society's 'Donovan Cup Competition' for unpublished work in October 1947. It also won the Jessie Mackay Memorial prize for verse in June 1948. This prize had been established the year of poet Jessie Mackay's death in 1938 by the New Zealand centre of the writers' organisation PEN. Mackay's work was included in a number of anthologies of New Zealand poetry which were produced in her lifetime, and in the anthology edited by Robert Chapman and Jonathan Bennett in 1956. But the DNZB entry on her states:

> However, her exclusion from the 1960 *Penguin book of New Zealand verse*, edited by Allen Curnow, limited awareness of her contribution to New Zealand literature among later generations of readers. Mackay's place in the history of New Zealand poetry has been considerably under-recognised. (Roberts, DNZB: website).

The Spring 1948 issue of the American literary magazine *Voices* No 133 also features Gilbert's work. In the selection of New Zealand poetry Gilbert leads, filling nearly two pages. The *Yearbook of the Arts in New Zealand* 1949, has Gilbert's poem 'Phobia', and her first full collection *Lazarus and Other Poems* was published by A.H. & A.W. Reed, Wellington, in 1949. Also in 1949 the *New Zealand Listener*[4] recorded that Gilbert won the 'Jessie Mackay Memorial prize' for poetry. She had in fact won the prize twice in successive years, 1948 and 1949, and would again in 1967, when she shared that year's prize with Baxter. In 1949 Gilbert began to contribute poems to the *New Zealand Listener* and did so up until March 1975; that is, she contributed during the years when Monte Holcroft was editor.

Gilbert states that when her book was published in London she had reviews not influenced by New Zealand literary politics, hence different from what she would have received in New Zealand. Gilbert said that she thought being a New Zealand woman writer of her period was a more difficult life than her male counterparts:

> Here you might be either over-praised or over-damned ... I think most male reviewers approach a piece of writing differently when they see a woman's name on it. They unconsciously patronise. A writer wants to be recognised as

---

[3] Brasch, in his 1962 publication, *Landfall Country* which was described on the dust jacket as being 'a remarkable picture of New Zealand achievement in literature and painting. Further, it offers a view of the emerging character of life here as seen through the eyes of the most perceptive writers and artists ...' Out of the 36 entries in the writers section, 5 were women. The artists fared somewhat better, with 10 pieces by women out of 22 art works.

[4] 11 November 1949, p9.

a writer, not as a man or a woman. But even when a woman writer becomes known, she is not the male writer's equal (Gilbert in Wright, 2007: 17-18).

Gilbert stated that she had three books of verse published by that time and her work had appeared in anthologies of New Zealand and Commonwealth verse and in periodicals in New Zealand, Australia, Canada and Ireland; her work had also been broadcast by the B.B.C. Gilbert explained:

> I am not prolific enough to be sending it out all over the place ... I don't sit down at a desk to write. With me it's a matter of waiting till I have something to say. Then anything may catch my eye and I'm away (Gilbert in Wright, 2007: 18).

With this outlook it's hardly surprising that Gilbert always liked the musical, lyrical and perhaps more traditional verse. She continued that this was her voice, not that she was against the moderns. Gilbert, who wrote verse from the age of about nine, kept black books with 'the most ghastly verse' and contributed to her school magazine. She was in her early 20s when a friend suggested she should show her verse to C.A. Marris. Marris, then writing in *The Evening Post* as Percy Flage, told her: 'You can write, but you mustn't send anything out till I tell you'. He got her work first into the Post, under the initial 'R', and later into *Art in New Zealand* and *New Zealand Best Poems*.

New Zealand Women Writers' Society
'Mr. Marris has been much criticised,' Gilbert says. 'But I feel he was genuinely interested in New Zealand literature and was only trying to get writers published'.[5] While Gilbert has always faced the hostility of some male writers, especially between 1943 and 1966, she was always highly respected among other women writers. In 1953 Gilbert appeared in *POEMS: Anthology by New Zealand Women Writers*, which was the first 'women only' poetry anthology to appear in New Zealand. Such an anthology was first proposed at the July 1942 AGM of the New Zealand Women Writers' Society 'a suggestion that the society publish a book for public sale was rejected as not opportune under the war conditions of the time'. The editor of the 1953 book, Alan R. Dunlop, stated in his introduction, 'it introduces to New Zealanders a body of poetry by writers so far largely unknown, and it marks one of the rare occasions in any country when women writers have published a volume devoted exclusively to their own poetry'.

Many male commentators were disparaging of the New Zealand WWS. Michael King, for example, in his biography of Janet Frame described them as a 'guild of largely (but not wholly) undistinguished authors and would-be authors'. However, Frame herself saw a different side of the Society and wrote in an introduction to a history of the New Zealand Women Writers' Society:

> I think the history is important. It is also important for me because my mother was one of the early writers – mostly women at home with a family – who gained such solace from the writers' society founded during the Depression. I think I have an early edition of the *Journal of the New Zealand Women's Writers' and Artists Society* ...' (Frame in Hayward & Cowley, 1982: 1).[6]

---

[5] Gilbert, R: newspaper article, 1966, 'Hard Lines for Women Writers.'

[6] Frame's mother Lottie Frame wrote poetry. According to King: 'One visitor [Majorie Hore] reported, in a horrified tone, that she had called upon "Mrs Frame" one afternoon and found her "sitting at the kitchen table, scribbling poetry on an envelope, surrounded by dirty dishes

As previously stated Curnow's 1951 revised edition of his groundbreaking anthology *A Book of New Zealand Verse* had 20 entries by men and 3 by women. It is interesting to conjecture that the women's anthology of the following year could be seen as a direct challenge to Curnow's anti-Georgian and anti-women writing, for he saw the two, Georgianism and femaleness, as being the same thing. A later anthology can also be compared with Curnow's to contrast the different male to female ratio of representation in literary collections. Robert Chapman & Jonathan Bennet's 1956 *An Anthology of New Zealand Verse* had 34 entries by men and 9 by women, one of whom was Gilbert – still a huge difference and an even greater one in absolute terms though somewhat more balanced in proportional terms.

It is interesting to note and contrast two books of poetry published in the year 1936 that seem to set the tone for the times to come in the post-war period through to the 1970s. *New Zealand Best Poems 1936* edited by C.A. Marris had poems by 9 women and 10 men, while *Verse Alive number two*, selected by H. Winston Rhodes and Denis Glover, had one woman and 10 men, and Robin Hyde is the only woman to appear in both. Nelson Wattie's article in *The Oxford Companion to New Zealand Literature* speaks of the contribution made to the furthering of New Zealand letters by the Christchurch and Auckland newspaper, *The Sun*, which existed from 1914 until 1934. This is important as it is at this juncture around 1935 that it appears the rift begins with the traditional, Georgian and therefore women poets. The newer, mostly male poets, saw themselves as progressive, bohemian, Modernist-masculinist poets, as opposed to the Georgian/female poets. Wattie quotes Pat Lawlor, who wrote in 1935 about *The Sun*:

> the pivot of its enterprise, its literary staff, was unequalled in the history of journalism in this country ... the poets, short-story writers and essayists *The Sun* has discovered and helped over the last two decades represent nearly every New Zealand writer who has achieved any distinction in his profession during that period (Lawlor in 'Oxford Companion', 1998: 520).[7]

Robin Hyde saw to *The Sun* as the one and only daily to pay any serious attention to literary work taken from the stores of New Zealand writers. The literary editors of *The Sun*, firstly Marris and then J.H.E Schroder, appear to have given equal time and space to both male and female writers.

A look at the list of writers to appear in the paper's Christmas editions each year sees the names of prominent writers of each sex. Hector Bolitho, Eileen Duggan, C.R. Allen, Robin Hyde, Monte Holcroft, Jane Mander and Will Lawson are all there. In an ironic twist Fairburn's poem for 1928: 'Kowhai' is as sentimentally Georgian as any of the poems he and his [masculinist] comrades were later to scorn. *The Sun* was the first daily to serialise the work of New Zealand novelists, for example, Edith Howe's *Young Pioneers* in 1923-1924, and it also has the distinction of having published the internationally renowned New Zealand author, Ngaio Marsh,

---

and flies – well ..." This was not "normal" behaviour in a New Zealand town in the 1930s where, even amid poverty, pretension and social ambition were rife, and women's domestic reputations were made or broken according to whether or not they scrubbed their front doorsteps' (King, 2000: 31).

[7] Lawlor was a supporter of women writers and 'chaired the first meeting of the [New Zealand Women's Writers'] Society [in 1932] convened by Nellie Donovan and until his death at the age of 86 in 1979, he kept up his interest and encouragement and was affectionately known as "the father of the Society" ... he was elected and Hon. Vice-President of our Society in 1977, the first [and only] male to hold this position' (France et al, 1982: 5).

including her first ever published story, 'The Night Train from Grey' in 1919. Many of the best-known New Zealand writers until the 1930s were women, for example, Katherine Mansfield, Jane Mander, Jean Devanny, Blanche Baughan, Eileen Duggan, Ursula Bethell. But the winds of change were afoot. In *Whole Men* Kai Jensen states:

> The group of young male writers that arose in the 1930s characterised this kind of writing [Georgian] as effeminate and claimed to offer a more down-to-earth, masculine alternative' (Jensen, 1996: 43).

Jensen adds that Sargeson identified Mansfield's use of metaphorical language with the 'feminine tradition' of fiction, and Glover stated that it was 'time to impart new vitality to New Zealand verse. No more leisurely–whimsy, feminine–mimsy stuff'. In 1937 Glover complained: 'Alas, New Zealand literature distils/an atmosphere of petticoats and frills' and Fairburn had grumbled to Glover in a letter in 1935 that 'the Menstrual School of Poetry is in the ascendant, and a mere male is treated with scant respect'.

Jensen points out that Curnow thought at this time that low standards of literary editing had allowed '[hobbyists] and ungifted amateurs' to be published, and in support noted that, of thirty-five new poets published in *Kowhai Gold*, eighteen were women, which he apparently regarded as a terrible indictment. H. Winston Rhodes, who in 1938 in the literary paper *Tomorrow* wrote: 'The beginnings of a national literature are to be found when writers turn to deal with the normal activities of ordinary men'. Perhaps there are no 'ordinary women'. Ironically, Quentin Pope, editor of *Kowhai Gold*, expressed the hope that its contents might serve as the foundation of a New Zealand literature, but within a few years the anthology was being seen as the embodiment of a moribund tradition of versifying, dominated by 'genteel female poets'.

Eileen Duggan

Peter Whiteford notes that prominent among the poets included in *Kowhai Gold* was Eileen Duggan, whose father, like Janet Frame's, was a railway worker and as such one of Rhodes' 'ordinary men'. Whiteford explains that Duggan:

> until then [the publication of *Kowhai Gold*] had enjoyed a reputation second to none. Internationally, her poetry continued to be well received, but in New Zealand her standing began to wane, and never recovered; a largely male, secular group of younger poets and critics, attracted by Modernist forms and philosophies, had little time for her more traditional lyrics, or for her active Catholicism. Her subsequent absence from major anthologies was as a result of her own decision, but it was a decision she felt forced to make by the prejudice and animosity she encountered (Whiteford, 2008: website, no pagination).

On the dust-jacket of Duggan's 1951 collection, *More Poems*, is a quote from a review of her work in the *Manchester Guardian* stating 'Our English [i.e. literature] anthologists will not have done their duty until they have brought in Miss Duggan's best'. It is conceivable that such statements from an overseas publication of high literary standing may have made Curnow increase his efforts to convince Duggan to allow her work in his anthology.

Poet Walter de la Mare's introduction to Duggan's 1937 book *Poems* drew attention to the freshness, incisiveness, and energy of the writing, and the presence of 'a unique feeling expressed in a renewed language', but even as her work was published, changes in literary fashion were reaching New Zealand that would ultimately see her and many other women writers marginalized within the New Zealand literary community. I have noted earlier that Glover, in *The Arraignment of Paris* decried the 'atmosphere of petticoats and frills'. Witty his verses may have been, but they were not good-natured, as McKay describes them, any more than was Fairburn's denigration of what he called 'the menstrual school' of poetry.

With their patronising and chauvinist stance, Glover and Fairburn felt a need to promote an alternative in New Zealand literature and this was effected partly by the publications of the Caxton Press, which Glover established and ran. In 1943, Curnow sought Duggan's permission to include some of her poems in the anthology he was preparing, published in 1945 by the Caxton Press, but she refused. In 1948, Curnow again sought permission to include her work when the anthology was being revised, but again she declined. Curnow's judgement of her work in his introduction that 'the whole effect is that of an emotional cliché' can hardly have encouraged her to participate. In a somewhat tetchy footnote to his discussion of Duggan in the same introduction Curnow notes: 'That is not to say there are not poems by Miss Duggan which I wished to include in this book; and they would have been included if she had not refused permission to reprint'. Peter Whiteford writes:

> Duggan continued to publish abroad and her reputation in England, Australia, and the United States remained high. However, something of the literary climate within which it was released may be gauged from an unpublished letter written by Fairburn to Charles Brasch, editor of *Landfall* at the time. Declining an invitation to review Duggan's 1951 *More Poems*, Fairburn was pleased to be relieved of 'the obligation to abuse a spinster. Duggan's verse has never been much more to me than a distant mewing: I haven't read this latest book, but should be surprised to find it much different in texture and feeling from what went before it'. It is a far cry from the letter Fairburn wrote to Duggan in 1929, describing 'And at the End' as 'one of the greatest things I've ever read'. Had Fairburn read the new work, he might indeed have been surprised, for the volume represents, as E.H. McCormick notes, 'a remarkable achievement, the transformation in late maturity of long-established poetic habits in response to the pressure of inner experience'. (Whiteford, 2008)

After the publication of *More Poems*, Duggan stopped writing verse. Although she continued to earn her living through her prose writing for another twenty years, her poetry was silenced. In certain respects, the development of New Zealand poetry in the middle years of the twentieth century was closely bound up with the emergence of Modernism and issues of nationalism. Eileen Duggan was as impassioned about New Zealand as any of the generation of writers succeeding her, but she cared little for and actively resisted the Modernist movement, an example of her ideas about them can be found in her parody 'Shades of Maro of Toulouse':

> Where are the words that broke the heart with beauty?
> This is the age of the merely clever ...
> [who] In one breath decry reason and avow it
> Demand it of others but claim to transcend it
> (Duggan, 1951: 17).

Whiteford contends that it may have been Duggan's misfortune to have been the last of the New Zealand pre-Modernist writers, but she was arguably also the most important, and most accomplished. Her subsequent absence from major anthologies was a result of her own decision, but it was a decision she felt forced to make by the prejudice and animosity she encountered. For Duggan the damage had been done and 'Shades of Maro of Toulouse' is a response to her 'clever' critics. This poem shows that Duggan was well versed in classical literature and her title 'Maro of Toulouse' echoes Virgil, sometimes known as Maro, who re-wrote 'Georgic' tales of idyllic settings, with echoes of Georgianism, is discussed later in this chapter in relation to the Georgian/Modernist debate. Duggan appears to be satiric when she advises her publisher to:

> Change the name of the poem, 'Shades of Virgilius Maro' to 'Shades of Maro of Toulouse', since it is not the great Virgil but Maro of Toulouse who wrote 'A Secret Latin for the Initiates' (Duggan in Whiteford, 1994: 150).

On October 22nd, 1972, the literary community was shocked by the sudden death of poet James K. Baxter, whose death was a prominent national news item. Six weeks later, on December 10th, 1972, Eileen Duggan died quietly in Wellington hospital, her death overshadowed by that of the younger male poet.

'Ordinary' men

T.H. Scott, in a long and much-cited essay in *Landfall* in the 1940s, backed by Rhodes and Monte Holcroft, held strong views about ordinary men. Scott argued that the works of New Zealand people were not 'scones, frocks or the raising of children, but houses, farms, roads, and bridges'. He did not comment on whether women enjoyed their role in having the babies, making the scones, and wearing the frocks. It is interesting to note here that, except perhaps for Glover during his wartime service in the merchant navy, none of these so-called 'ordinary men' had stereotypically masculine occupations.

Most of these men were teachers, university lecturers or public service office workers: that is, they all had middle-class professional occupations. Jensen points out that when Scott writes of 'New Zealanders' he is thinking of 'New Zealand men'. Meanwhile, poet and historian Keith Sinclair would look back on Scott's essay as 'a kind of manifesto ... [that] made a powerful impression on some of us at the time'. So the stage was set in the 1930s for the battle between the sexes of the New Zealand literary scene in the post-war period. Gilbert and Curnow were miles apart. For him she was the archetypal woman poet, and as such he appears to have detested her.

Wright considers Gilbert was badmouthed by Curnow from 1947 onward, having been omitted from his anthologies and poorly treated by people under Curnow's influence, such as the early C. K. Stead and the early Vincent O'Sullivan, whose 1970 *An Anthology of New Zealand Poetry* seems flawed by her omission. Critics like C A Marris, John Schroder, Monte Holcroft, Denis Glover in private, Louis Johnson, Frank McKay. Peter Smart, Ian Wedde, Jenny Bornholdt, Terry Locke, Lauris Edmond, Joan Stevens, James Bertram, Riemke Ensing, and Helen Shaw all attested to Gilbert's merits, a better coverage of critical opinion than most local poets can claim.

Kite, the newsletter of the Association of New Zealand Literature, has under the editorship of Heather Murray only ever referred to Ruth Gilbert critically and Wright believes this is due to the lingering influence and authority of Curnow in its editorial circle. Wright stated he had praised Johnson as a critic and editor, but found his biggest lapse concerned Gilbert in 1957. Johnson published poems by both Macky and Gilbert in the *New Zealand Poetry Yearbook* of that year. However, the poem Johnson quotes in full is also in his bitter criticism of *The Sunlit Hour* in *numbers 6*. Wright notes that Gilbert also appears in *New Zealand Poetry Yearbook* Volume 7, 1957-58 with a poem later than *The Sunlit Hour*.

numbers

Even in the pre-1964 period the Wellington group without exception slowly surrendered their very obvious Georgian affinities. The first issue of a new literary review edited by Johnson, *numbers 1*, in July 1954 seemed to represent a changed attitude to the prevailing anti-women stance of the time. In a review of four recently published poems by women poets 'Women, God Bless 'Em' the reviewer 'Scruto' proclaims: 'There was a time, not long ago, when the price of serious writing in New Zealand – especially among women – was likely to be paid by way of dementia or at least ostracism'.

But, by 1957, as is apparent in Johnson's hostile review in *numbers 6*, March 1957 of Gilbert's *The Sunlit Hour* (1956), her first book of poems since 1949, Johnson seems to have fallen in line with Curnow's critical anti-Georgian stance. Johnson was as disrespectful in his *numbers 6* review, to which Willow Macky responded in *numbers 7*. Johnson's review is evidence of the disputes discernible in the male/female poetic politics during the period.[8]

Macky's criticism of Johnson's review appeared in her letter to *numbers 7* followed by Johnson's reply.[9] This battle seems to be at the nub of the differences I argue existed between men and women writers during the period, notwithstanding the fact that Johnson was one of the more sympathetic and supportive writers and publishers towards women writers. In 'Controversy: The Critic On The Mat' in *numbers 7* Macky wrote:

> the New Zealand reviewer is not in question, but it is obvious that they are almost completely lacking in understanding with regard to the woman writer – a fault far more evident in New Zealand than overseas (Macky, *Numbers 7*, 1957: 26).

Thus, even a sympathetic male like Johnson is seen by Macky as showing little understanding towards women writers.

It is interesting to note Gilbert's career after the 1950s. My analysis is informed by Wright's studies of her work. He notes that 'her poems appeared in the *Anthology of Commonwealth Verse*' (Wright, 2007: 10). Gilbert was a member of the New Zealand centre of the writers' organisation P.E.N. since 1950, was a past president, represented P.E.N. on the State Literary Fund Committee, and represented New Zealand at an international writer's congress in Dublin in 1953. American academic, Phyllis Ann French, writing a thesis on New Zealand women poets in the 1960s in 1967, 'Twelve Women Poets of New Zealand: imperatives of shape and growth', included Gilbert.

Wright suggests, as a comment on the sex-poetry battle that by the mid-1960s there may have been a cooling off as both men and women of the previous era came under threat from a new generation.[10] He argues:

---

[8] See Appendix 11 for the full text of Johnson's review.

[9] See Appendix 12 for the full text of Macky's letter and Johnson's reply.

[10] Even later anthologies, in so-called liberated times, have tended to consolidate this difference. For example, Brunton, Edmond & Leggott, *Big Smoke (New Zealand Poems 1960 to 1975)* had 38 entries by men and 18 by women. This was even more pronounced in Arthur Baysting's 1973 anthology *The Young New Zealand Poets* which had 18 male poets and only 1 female poet, Jan Kemp.

in 1967 the 'Jessie Mackay Prize' was shared between Ruth Gilbert for *The Luthier* and James K. Baxter for *Pig Island Letters*. You can say therefore that down to that date a balance was being maintained and even a reconciliation was promoted by the powers that be. In fact the Baby Boom generation was just then arriving on the scene and while neither Baxter nor Gilbert was driven off the scene they were no longer centre stage. Baxter died in 1972 after a few years of his greatest public standing as a poet (Wright, 2007: 21-22).

Before her third 'Jessie Mackay Prize' was awarded Gilbert wrote to Wright in 1966 about the reviews of her book *The Luthier*. In the letter she stated:

> I have been pleased with my 'Listener' Review & not surprised at all by Louis Johnson's opinion in 'The Dominion'. Poor old Lou! I would need to change my sex to please him! (Gilbert in 'Among', 2007: 11).

Gilbert and Johnson appear to have become friends again later. Gilbert's work from the 1970s onwards and other commentaries reveal a life dedicated to poetry. At least Joan Stevens in the 1970 *Contemporary Poets of the English Language*, of which James Bertram was the New Zealand editor, endorsed her work.

Helen Shaw's anthology *Mystical Choice* (1981) includes Gilbert as did the selections of New Zealand poetry Helen Shaw guest edited in overseas literary magazines such as *The Japonica Sings*, May 1979. In *The Journal of New Zealand Literature* article by John Needham on 'Recent Poetry and Coleridgean Principles' examines the poetry of Gilbert. Her work was included in the *Penguin Book of New Zealand Verse*, edited by Ian Wedde and Harvey McQueen.

In 1985 Wright published his survey of Gilbert's published poetry in *Ruth Gilbert: An Account of Her Poetry*, written as a review of her *Collected Poems* and included her annotations. Wright has since written a series of essays and notes commenting on Gilbert's career and poetry. In Mary Paul's review in the *Listener*, 11 February, 1987, of *Yellow Pencils*, an anthology by Lydia Wevers, Paul asks why, if the anthology is meant to be inclusive, is Gilbert, who is still writing and publishing and has been in all the other anthologies, excluded?

In the *Dominion*, 18 September 1990, there was a letter to the editor by Gilbert defending Sylvia Ashton-Warner against a detractor who had referred to Ashton-Warner as 'selfish, arrogant, snobbish and anti-social'. She wrote: 'To those of us who knew her best, she remains what she always was: a warm, compassionate woman, an admired writer, and a loved and loving friend'. It is interesting to note here that Ashton-Warner, in a 1967 letter to Gilbert, who had sent her a copy of her newly published *The Luthier*, wrote: 'I saw Louis Johnson's review in *The Star*. (Akld.) But whenever I see a review in N.Z. that is less than favourable ... I suspect a good book behind it ...'[11]

From 1990 onwards Gilbert's work has begun to appear in more anthologies. They reflect the longevity of her poetry despite this earlier belittling by male critics and publishers of the 1950s and 1960s. *The Feminist Companion to English Literature* includes an entry on Gilbert.[12] Gilbert's daughter, Deirdre Mackay, a reporter for the *Nelson Mail*, and author, wrote a lengthy profile of her mother (1991). Mackay gives an outline of her mother's literary life and her literary relationship with Ashton-Warner, Wright, Holcroft and Glover.[13]

---

[11] See for relevant remarks also WHENUA: the letters of Sylvia Ashton-Warner to Ruth Gilbert 1967-1984, available in the Turnbull Library.

[12] Copy of article in Wright 2002/H. Though cited, Wright was not its author.

Gilbert's publishing career continued and her *Complete Early Poems, 1938-1944: with six later pieces* were published by Original Books in Wellington in 1994. An anthology of love poems, *My Heart Goes Swimming*, compiled by Jenny Bornholdt and Gregory O'Brien in 1996, includes Gilbert. She appeared in *The Oxford Anthology of New Zealand Poetry in English* (1997) edited by Bornholdt, O'Brien and Mark Williams. *The Oxford Companion to New Zealand Literature* (1998) has an entry on Ruth Gilbert by Wright, who also published her *Complete Sappho Poems* in the same year.

One ironic aspect of Gilbert's career, domestic and literary, that brought her two worlds together happened at this time. In 1998 the tissue firm Snowtex issued 'The Poetry Series' on its packages, with a quote from Shelley and poems by Wordsworth, Gilbert, Katherine Mansfield and Shakespeare, putting Gilbert on a par with Mansfield, and both New Zealand women in the company of Britain's greatest poets. Gilbert appeared in Terry Locke's *Jewels in the Water: contemporary New Zealand poetry for younger readers*, published in 2000 and his anthology *Doors: a Contemporary New Zealand Poetry Selection* (2000) on which Wright commented to Gilbert as follows:

> I have looked at Terry Locke's *Doors*. You will not have missed that [at 84] you are the oldest contributor, by four years with Rosalie Carey next. So it is indeed something that you appear in an anthology of CONTEMPORARY poetry in 2000. In fact it is pretty representative of poets publishing and active in the 1990's (Wright, 2007: 28-29).

In 2002 Gilbert was awarded Officer of the New Zealand Order of Merit for poetry. Anne Else (in *Landfall* 1985: 431-446) addresses the treatment reviewers gave to Gilbert. Gilbert turned 90 in 2007, and while she faced hostility from some male writers from 1943-1966, she was always respected among women writers.[14]

Glover, Fairburn, Baxter

Commenting on an oft-quoted epigram of Denis Glover's, Jensen writes:

> I have several times heard Glover's deplorable jibe, 'Women poets: a bunch of bores in stuffy drawers', quoted as though definitive of his misogyny – yet he scrawled it on the back of the envelope in which he had just received an angry letter from Robin Hyde … It's arguable, also, that Fairburn's and Glover's anti-feminist statements were part of the founding stage of their literary movement … they mark the development of a literary culture in which women writers did not prosper; yet they are not typical. Perhaps the basic problem with either

---

[13] Deirdre Mackay writes: A bonus from writing (i.e. her mother's writing) was the friendships with other writers and publishers which developed with time. 'We used to visit Denis Glover at Paekakariki and had hilarious afternoons discussing writers and writing. Denis was a wonderful mimic and would have everyone laughing.' She (Ruth Gilbert) and Denis had more serious discussions about the nature of poetry too. [Gilbert says] 'We agreed that what makes a poem is magic. This can't be defined but you know it when you find it.' Thus, despite often overtly sexist proclamations by Glover et al the men and women poets found common ground at times.

[14] e-mail correspondence between the American poet, Cameron La Follette and Niel Wright in the 'Cameron La Follette'.

sex role theory or a monolithic patriarchal conspiracy is that neither theory reflects the complexity of human experience (Jensen, 1996: 9-10).

Chris Hilliard recalls that the scholars, critics, historians, librarians and literary lawyers were crucial gatekeepers of poetic taste and New Zealand's historical awareness 1920-1950, acting as go-betweens for writers, publishers and the New Zealand reading public. He also makes interesting use of international commentators on the New Zealand literary scene. For example, Hilliard writes:

> The Australian critic Nettie Palmer championed [Eileen] Duggan, Jessie Mackay, and Katherine Mansfield in four separate articles from 1927 to 1930. Her husband, Vance Palmer, also praised Mackay, Duggan and Blanche Baughan ('there are no women writing more authentic poetry in English today'), as well as Mansfield and Mander. 'To an outsider,' he remarked, 'the most remarkable thing about Maoriland writing is the originality and strength of the women and the relative feebleness of the men (Hilliard, 2006: 35).

Hilliard's words suggest that there is no sign that 'Georgian' poetry had any connotations of effeminacy and the poetry of Jessie Mackay certainly did not seem soppy or twee to any bookman. Only the judgements and rhetoric of the next generation of 'literary men' would make the Georgian tradition seem 'feminine'. However, even now the perceptions of Georgianism are still negative and they sometimes appear 'in reviews to disparage those who write in ways regarded for the moment or from the perspective of the reviewer as old-fashioned' (Robinson, 1998: 200).

As opposed to the perceptions of women writers, the male writers of the 1940s, 1950s and the 1960s were prone to present themselves as practical men: as gardeners, printers, handymen. They liked to talk about writing as work or craft. Male writers projected the image of a masculine literature by their emphasis on hearty drinking. Jensen describes how Glover recalled the old Paekakariki Pub on the Kapiti Coast north of Wellington with considerable reverence, as a link in the chain of male drinking institutions, hotels and the like throughout the country and the world when he was in the Merchant Navy during WW2.

In fact, Glover is quoted in his memoir as saying, somewhat romantically, nostalgically, and a trifle disingenuously: 'One must regret those days, when there were no women [in the pub], no altercations, no knives or bottle-bashings ...' Sargeson recalled the 1951 Writers' Conference as 'all very enlivening: literary chatter, politics, anecdotes: the full range from bawdy stories to learned epigrams that accompanied the beer in the out-of-the-way after-hours pub'. Jensen asks how many writers in these after-hours pub sessions were women? The answer is probably none, but if there were did they inhibit the bawdiness of the stories? Could the few women writers who appear in the 1951 conference photograph participate fully in its life as described above by Sargeson? Jensen quotes Glover's poem 'To a woman shopping':

> What's death to the lady, pray?
> Even shopping's a bore
> - The carcasses gently sway
> As she goes out the door
>
> But death goes with her on her way
> In her basket along the street
> Rolls heavily against her thigh
> The blood-red bud of the meat

Notwithstanding the sexual innuendo of the last two lines, would Glover write a poem about a man going to buy meat at the butchers? The subjects of death, meat and carcasses leads to the topic of male violence in New Zealand literature.

Kendrick Smithyman, discussing New Zealand poetry in 1965, quoted Lionel Trilling on the 'powerful and obsessive significance that violence has for the intellectual'. It's likely the intellectual he has in mind is male, and for New Zealand male intellectuals in the mid-twentieth century, death and violence were of particular interest for their masculine connotations. Literature that focused on these topics could present itself as a serious business, the work of 'responsible adult New Zealanders'.

Another topic that could be said to characterise the new literature was that of the 'man alone'. Baxter suggested this was the distinguishing mark of the 1930s and 1940s. In his 1954 lecture series, later published as *The Fire and the Anvil*, he wrote:

> The anxiety, however, which accompanies the taking on of this role is a different matter. It seems to derive from the artist's awareness that his activity is regarded with indifference or even hostility by the society in which he lives. The symbol of *Man Alone* is thus objectified as the hobo, the social outcast, standing for the outcast energies, both criminal and creative, which the artist tries to reintegrate in his view of the world. (Baxter, 1957: 72).

Fairburn appears to turn these arguments upside down by claiming that:

> Women have little or no moral courage, because they do not understand what it means; just as men are, on the whole, deficient in biological courage ... a man will always be tempted to consider sensual enjoyment, or the accumulation of power, or (more rarely) self-sacrifice to an idea, as being at least as important as the pursuit of simple biological ends. The normal woman is never in doubt about such things. It is the abnormal woman, the blue-stocking or male impersonator of some kind or other, who (under masculine influence of some sort) can interest herself in the things of the spirit (Fairburn, 1967: 20).

The irony of putting the Baxter and Fairburn quotes together is that they show up the male poet's difficulty in attempting to accommodate the female element or the female person in life and literature.

From Baxter's understanding it would appear that women represent the 'social norm', whereas in Fairburn it looks as if the female element is the untamed and amoral member of society, and men are the reasoned, intellectual and spiritual 'higher beings'. These ideas of women can be found elsewhere in the male literary litany of American and European thought at this time of the early and mid-twentieth century. For example, E. Fuller Torrey on Ezra Pound states: 'Pound's prose and poetry written during the Rapallo years [1920s and 1930s] enlarged on the sexual theories he had previously explored. Woman is viewed as a primitive creature, a kind of primordial biological receptacle'.

> Chiefist of these the second, the female
> Is an element, the female
> Is a chaos
> An Octopus
> A biological process

and we seek to fulfil ...

. . . .

She is a submarine, she is an octopus, she is
A biological process
(Pound in Torrey, 1984: 128).

However, some poetry written by men was at the heart of their criticism of others. For example, what Jensen refers to as one of Fairburn's 'limpist' epigrams, 'Any-Book-of-the-Month-Club':

The virgin marks her calendar
and still goes undefiled
she menstruates most regular
and never has a child
(Fairburn in Jensen, 1996: 89).

This negative comment on women writers and readers groups, and on spinsters, was admired by literary critic James Bertram: '[If] any New Zealand epigram deserves to stand with the best of Roy Campbell', wrote Bertram, 'it is surely [this one]'. Baxter admired the bawdiness and irreverence of Fairburn's and Glover's lighter verse and of prose writers who tried to suggest the bawdiness of slang in all-male situations; in war literature this was taken a lot further. Also, in rugby changing rooms, both bawdiness and homophobia are dealt with, along with issues of Māori and Pākehā relations.

There seems little place for women in either the literary or real lives of these artists and human beings. As Jensen points out, alongside the 'manly' qualities of rough talk and expressing the language of ordinary workers, soldiers etc. this group also put great store in writing being both literary and intellectual, which equated with masculinity. He points out that Curnow and others claimed good writing was defined by intellect. Curnow admired the 'masculine erudition' of Wallace Stevens. Fairburn observed that Eileen Duggan and other Georgian, that is women, writers were 'highly competent, but lacking in any one of the essential qualities that make good poetry – brains, bile, guts and so on'.

Wealth of vocabulary and deftness in using difficult forms [of poetry] were also described in terms of masculinity. In his literary satire *The Arraignment of Paris* Glover compares the effeminate poets of the *Best Poets* group with his own, more manly poetry comrades who can:

... leap a five-barred gate of rhyme
and still keep on whistling all the time
while Paris and his valiant spinster crew
assault a common stile and then cry 'Phew!'
(Glover, 1981: 11)

Jensen concludes that the male writers used metaphors to describe literary attributes such as vigour, strength (key nouns), rough, robust (key adjectives). In contrast bad writing was weak, slack, feeble, sickly. He says that Fairburn seemed to lose the distinction between metaphors of masculine physique and the reality that good writing might be produced by frail or homosexual men, or by women, and Fairburn went so far as to say that most of the love songs written in the previous twenty years suggested either impotence or homosexuality (there is no mention of women here at all).

While discussing a poem in Baxter's *Blow, Wind of Fruitfulness* Curnow noted 'a welcome gain in irony and detachment, a more muscular growth in Mr Baxter's thought'. Curnow, in an introduction to R.A.K. Mason's *Collected Poems* admired 'the supple movement of their syntax, the muscle and bone of a living speech, they waken the mind to share the unique vision of a poet'. Thus the negative version of the above becomes weakness, slightness or fatness. In his attack on Louis Johnson's 1952 *Poetry Yearbook* Curnow says it is a 'fatty degeneration of the verse, lacking in nerve and sinew'. According to Curnow, 'nineteenth century New Zealand poetry was the voice of Alfred Lord Tennyson, thinned and grown womanish', another derogatory remark equating femaleness with weakness.

The Masculinists differentiated their own 'male' literature by trying to characterize New Zealand literature of the previous period as being effeminate and having been mainly written by women. And while it is true that many of New Zealand's best writers in the first three decades of the twentieth century were women (Mansfield, Mander, Devanny, Baughan, Bethell, Duggan) it did not translate into a preponderance of women writers in terms of numbers.

For example, Lauris Edmond counts women as being fewer than half of the contributors to Marris's 1934 *Best Poems* series, and about a third of the 1935 edition, and in Quentin Pope's *Kowhai Gold* it was roughly half-and-half. Despite these figures Glover felt it necessary to depict Marris (Paris) as an effeminate male leading a troupe of women through a 'tough' landscape they knew nothing about and Sargeson also used satire to belittle the 'Lady Poet'. Curnow argued against the inclusion of '[hobbyists] and amateurs' observing that eighteen out of thirty-five new contributors had been women, thus equating amateurism with female gender.

Summing up the male writers' attitudes during this period, Jensen argues they sought to generate a powerful, realistic masculine literature – at the cost of contemporary women writers, and of women in general, and that the *Tomorrow* and *Phoenix* magazines laid much of the foundations for the masculinists' philosophy to flourish, along with the introduction of the Caxton Press. Fairburn begins taunting the Georgians by satirizing the *Kowhai Gold* anthology – 'the bloom of the Kowhai has fallen, girls/did somebody give it a push?'. These attitudes grew through the 1930s and 1940s until, in 1950, Brasch was talking of 'those would-be poets, most of them long since silent, withered no doubt by that cold blast of reality the depression, whose work was collected in an anthology called *Kowhai Gold*'.

The masculinists had the advantage of the kind of close-knit, supportive community that feminist writers, Māori writers and post-modern text-art writers have enjoyed in recent decades and the masculinists were all enthusiastic young men who were excited by what they were doing. However, the downside of their enthusiasm is seen in Curnow's continuation of his defensive criticism long after the need, and by the end of the 1960s things were about to change. Evans in his *Penguin History of New Zealand Literature* notes that:

> For middle-class males of that post-war generation, literature was a heritage, something they came to naturally around the middle of the Sixties and began to use without question ... But for women and for Māori and for Māori women, the literary heritage was something that belonged to men. 'In the 50s and 60s, while other writers of my generation were sharing their experiments and publishing one another's work,' said Lauris Edmond (1924), a writer who began publishing in her fifties, 'I was living in country towns completely involved in bringing up my large family' (Evans, 1990: 215).

The evidence presented in this chapter suggests that the women poets of the post-war era, from 1945 to 1970 were disadvantaged simply by being women. The example of Gilbert and the disparaging attitude towards her as a poet and the resentment this engendered in her and other women of the period towards their male counterparts illustrates this. Remarks by many of the male poets towards women writers cannot be shrugged off as mere playfulness or banter but it may be argued that they portray a distrust and misogyny within the male literary fraternity. Because the male writers at the time were also often the editors and publishers of the literary magazines and journals, and therefore the gatekeepers of style and content, their attitudes towards the women poets and writers affected whether those women were published.

Chapter 6

Women Novelists

This chapter considers the background to the period 1945-1970 of the ideas and realities experienced by women writers of prose. It explores the effects of World War Two on the psyche of the male writers in the post-war period, looking at some of the underlying resentments and frustrations of returning soldiers and the effects these may have had on men's attitudes towards women. I then consider the writing careers of five women and discuss the effect of some prevailing attitudes on their writing styles and careers generally. I discuss each author to assess whether aspects of their personal lives, their family backgrounds and beliefs contributed to their literary ambitions.

The chapter includes Rosemary Rees, Ngaio Marsh, Dorothy Quentin, Dorothy Eden, Janet Frame, and mentions other women writers of fiction. Despite assumptions that women were not prominent in the 1940s to 1970s period, it appears at first that these women novelists were among the most successful New Zealand writers of the period both in terms of commercial success and literary note. They were among the most prolific in terms of numbers of publications, works translated into other languages, numbers of editions, and serialisation of individual titles, and began to supersede their male counterparts in these areas. However, while this may seem contradictory to my argument it will be seen that such achievements during the period were mainly recognised and realised overseas, Frame being an exception. But many of the women writers, such as Marsh, felt they were not taken seriously in New Zealand despite international recognition and success.

Until the 1940s men and women shared a reasonably equal publishing ratio in New Zealand, sometimes only one or two titles separating them in terms of numbers of books published within any given year or decade, although up until the 1920s the men tended to dominate. From the 1920s onwards through to the 1970s there is not one decade when women novelists did not outdo men in terms of publication numbers, although within some years this tended to move either way. The 1960s saw the widest gap in numbers, with women having 180 works of fiction published to the 134 published by men. However, in 1961 there were 4 books by women and 9 by men, and in 1967 12 by women and 13 by men. The overall picture of the decade is clear, yet it did not translate into critical acclaim or literary acceptance.

The effect of WW2

Jensen writes that the farmer and the workingman distilled a new national identity, but were also potential readers, who might recognize in the new writing 'their own authentic voice'. Excited by this hope, male writers of the day emphasized the hidden sensitivity and potential literacy of the practical man. For example, Sargeson described his uncle, Oakley Sargeson, as highly perceptive and noted that, although he was a struggling farmer with only primary school education, he was better read than Sargeson himself at that time.[15]

Jensen discusses WW2 and how 'it seemed that the war gave a powerful boost to the new male writers'. In 1945 Caxton published a short story anthology edited by Sargeson, *Speaking for ourselves*. Frame in her autobiography would record how, on reading this book at the close of the war, she felt 'the excitement of being in a land that was coming alive with its own writing, *speaking for itself*, with many of the writers returning from the war, bringing their urgency of experience'.

---

[15] I have noticed this myself over the years when I worked on the Railways and as a drain-layer: I have met other men who were far more well read than university people that I knew, perhaps because academics often restrict their interests to particular fields of knowledge.

It is assumed that wartime urgency of experience could be brought back only by male writers. This was not strictly true as most of the nurses looking after the wounded were women, who would have seen much of the consequences of the war on people despite not having been involved in the fighting. However, some war literature was the result of misogynist thought. One example already mentioned is Guthrie Wilson's novel, *Brave Company*, where a nurse suggests that the battle for Casino was a failure by New Zealand Division troops, where Wilson comments on this character:

> This of all insults is the least forgivable. Casino is very much a bitter and painful memory, not of defeat, but of costly frustration.
> 'The bitch should be strangled!' is Donald's solution.
> But Mitchison would accord her a useful death the nature of which cannot be here recorded (Wilson, 1962: 100).

The vitriolic reply to her accusations when the men are alone infers that she should be raped to death for her insults. Thus, 'Masculine' activities and disclaimers of literary status were two characteristic behaviours of male writers in the 1930s and 1940s and a masculine mythology was burgeoning in the literary community, as writers sought to close the gap between themselves and ordinary or manly New Zealand men. Writing itself had to be masculinized, in both material and style.

By 1940 the masculine literary movement had arrived, both in poetry and prose. Jensen argues that the beginning of the prose 'revolution' vis-à-vis the masculinist movement may have actually been started by Sargeson copying the style of a one page story published in the first issue of *Tomorrow* magazine, and that the story was by a woman writer, Alice M. Henderson. In his autobiography Sargeson gives credence to this possibility. He writes:

> Whether it was chance or influence or both I do not know, but about the time of my meeting with Fairburn I saw a copy of *Tomorrow* for the first time, and immediately wrote something which I could very surely recognise as quite different from anything I had written previously ... (Sargeson, 1981: 180).

After forging a new style of writing by 'combining form, style and range of material to suit a developing literary milieu, Sargeson's stories were heavily influential on other New Zealand writers of prose fiction: David Ballantyne, John Reece Cole, Davin, Finlayson, Gaskell'.

It is ironic that Sargeson, hailed as the first New Zealander to write as a real 'New Zealand Man' was a male homosexual and that he seems to have copied the original style and idea from a woman writer. It was Sargeson's use of colloquial New Zealand bar room working 'man's' language that, according to Fairburn, had given New Zealand literature something of the 'normal' New Zealander. Copland was amazed to find in Sargeson 'the mother tongue of Waipukurau and Eketahuna'. In 1948 Sargeson referred to Mansfield as 'very much indeed in the feminine tradition' which he equated with 'the *minor* tradition ... a tendency to be concerned with the part rather than the whole' and Dan Davin through his character Cody, says of KM 'She's a bit doll's house for me. The scale's too small'. That Mansfield is considered one of our finest and best-known writers, both in New Zealand and internationally, is dismissed.

Examples of the common tongue in poetry of ordinary people [that is, men] by Curnow and Glover are seen as progress from the 'lofty heights' of feminine/Georgian language, while a group of feminist critics, less sympathetically, talk of 'that harsh, laconic, bitten-off masculine dialect that Sargeson and Mulgan ... installed as the dominant discourse of New Zealand fiction'. Thus, both poetry and prose were affected by the masculinist philosophy. In fact, the whole of New Zealand literary expression appears to be under this masculinist influence. In Denys Trussell's biography of Fairburn he says that 'Literary' was almost a dirty word in Fairburn's correspondence with Glover. However, Fairburn praised Jane Mander as being worth any four other literary women in this country. He said of her that she's a woman; and she's not 'literary'.

As already alluded to, male writers of the period were at pains to identify with men who worked at manual labour. Thus, large groups of working men constituted the desired masculine location. For example, Bertram observed of Davin's novel *Roads from Home* that the New Zealand Railways plays a part not unlike that of the New Zealand Division in the war stories, a brotherhood of tough workingmen whose daily tasks involve strength, courage and the continual risk of sudden death or disabling accident.[16] And in Bill Pearson's novel *Coal Flat* the miners' union is yet another vision of healthy masculine community, a welcome contrast to Ma Palmer's overwhelming dominance of the family at the pub. As Davin indicates, it was the language of the soldier and the football team, thus the world of ordinary men:

> In the Irish way, and in the way of gregarious writers everywhere, he had always made much use of alcohol and pubs, was at home in them sometimes more than it seemed than he was at home. He never sought an exclusively literary company ... He liked men of strength and courage, hard men. But often in these later years the hard men were the hard drinkers. (Davin, 1985: 59)

War literature was an extreme version of the overall tendency to depict women as outside literary concerns. Fairburn argues that equality between the sexes 'was a 'sentimental' and 'romantic' heresy, spread by feminists and homosexuals'. Even when considered as satirical, this stance underlines a misogynist attitude, as previously he thought that women are inherently immoral and anti-social, that they have little notion of abstract justice and are incapable of principles. Women, he says, can act without moral consideration and are irrational:

> maintaining an objective and disinterested habit of thought [was difficult enough for a man] for women it is almost impossible ... Women's minds are not designed for the purpose of making judgements on matters that call for objective consideration ... [Women who had] acquired certain masculine habits of mind, through their association with intelligent men [might be] most charming, [but were] usually marginal creatures in the book of Genesis (Fairburn, 1967: 18-20).

Although Glover and Fairburn represent the extreme ideals of the 'masculinists' their aggressively masculine postures served the group purpose of making literature seem masculine. Summing up the male writers' attitudes during most of the period this thesis covers, Jensen thinks male writers sought to 'generate a powerful, realistic masculine literature – at the cost of contemporary women writers, and of women in general'.

Curnow, in a review of Pearson's *Coal Flat*, attacked Ashton-Warner's main character in *Spinster*, as 'the ... egomaniac Vorontosov rhapsody' (Curnow, 1963). Jensen notes that of the two it is Ashton-Warner's novel that stands the test of time

---

[16] Again I can attest to the reality of this feeling in the work I have done on the Railway track gang and laying sewer pipes etc. While most of these male writers did not experience these things themselves the authenticity of their writing about it is nonetheless true as they probably picked up the stories they wrote of in hotel conversations where they got their experience as "real men".

and that his attack emphasises Curnow's blind spot when it came to reviewing books that didn't fit into the masculinist theory. He regards Ashton-Warner's novel as having 'more staying power, even though it describes the interior life of an aging, alcoholic woman'.

The idea that male writers should identify with the ordinary man began to develop another side that showed a certain disenchantment with this stance. C.K. Stead tells a story of when Maurice Duggan was with literary friends in a bar a Māori man came up and said: 'You a Kiwi, mate?' Duggan responded with 'Yes mate, are you?'. Thus the writer challenged an ordinary working man (a Māori at that) on the idea of national identity. If the writer had needed to become more masculine, the ordinary man had to become more emotionally expressive.

To the writers and intellectuals the 'real men' weren't playing ball. Pearson wrote of the intolerance of the 'ordinary man' towards artists, who sought to enrich New Zealand society. Pearson argued:

> When the man-in-the-pub speaks his feelings he reduces them to a common denominator; he avoids distinction and definition in expression; tragedy is 'tough luck', disappointment 'a bit of a bastard' (Pearson, 1962: 342).

Implicit in Pearson's discussion is the idea of the artist as heroic, as being more masculine than other men, who are effeminate because they submit to convention. The above shows a confused aspect of the male writers' position.

Romance writing by women has often been portrayed as inferior and of slight literary worth. Of the five following case studies, three of the women can be classed as romance writers. However, outward appearances can be deceiving. American academic, Janice Radway, in her 1984 ground breaking study of 'Romance' books, *Reading the Romance*, analyzes the genre by examining the language of the romance novel and how that language affects the readers. Among those who have disparaged romance reading are feminists, literary critics, and theorists of mass culture who claim that romances reinforce the woman reader's dependence on men and acceptance of the repressive ideology purveyed by popular culture. Radway was the first serious writer to question such claims, arguing that critical attention 'must shift from the text itself, taken in isolation, to the complex social event of reading'.

She examines the complicated business of publishing in one of the most lucrative categories in the industry and its distribution, to the individual reader's engagement with the text. The style, Radway points out, is relatively simplistic. She describes it as dominated by cliché, simple vocabulary and standard syntax, and compares it to the nineteenth-century realist novel. Unlike New Zealand academic Joan Stevens, however, who sees this as a fault with romance writing, Radway argues that these methods allow romance novels to be easily read, and are not just a sacrificing of artistic ability. Thus the successful, fulfilling romance novel exists, she continues, when the author herself has provided meaning for her story through the words she has written. In an introduction to the 1987 British edition of her book, republished in "Reading *Reading the Romance*", Radway discussed the women she interviewed for her original book:

> They repeatedly explained their reading as a way of temporarily refusing the demands associated with their role as wives and mothers; they said that romance reading functioned as a 'declaration of independence', as a way of securing privacy while at the same time providing companionship and conversation. In this way, I unpack the significance of the word 'escape' ... The simple act of reading a book serves as a way of declaring themselves off-limits. I try to make the case for seeing romance reading as a form of resistance to a

situation predicated on the assumption that women alone are responsible for the care and the emotional nurturance of others. For them, romance reading creates a feeling of hope ... How did the heroine's experience foster their ability to see the heroine's story as interesting and how did it account for their willingness to see their own pleasure through the heroine's at the moment when they were directly confronting their dissatisfaction with traditionally structured heterosexual relationships? (Radway, 1997: 71).

Mary Scott, Joyce West & Nelle Scanlan

In her 1961 study of the New Zealand novel, Stevens writes that the 'basic defect of light fiction is, of course, that its development is according to pattern'. She goes on to imply that this kind of writing lacks development of plot and character and its main aim is to fulfil the need of the popular market. She concludes that while such works may be quietly perceptive and amusing, they deal 'exclusively with personal relationships within a feminine world, they are aimed at readers not minded to struggle with intellectual concepts or difficult imaginative pressures'. This idea of 'feminine thought' being somehow lightweight and inconsequential appears to be the underwritten criticism of the period, even from another woman and particularly from the masculinists.

However, Stevens and to a certain extent J.C. Reid, deserve some credit for being among the first literary academics in New Zealand universities to actually encourage discussion on New Zealand literature. However, the fact that Reid's book was self-published and Stevens' was essentially published with a non-university audience in mind, indicates that studying New Zealand literature was seen as somehow low-brow or not worthy of serious discussion.

The same can be said for the teaching of New Zealand history at the time and even until quite recently historians took little interest in New Zealand social history. Historian Jock Phillips, in acknowledging this lack before the 1990 New Zealand sesquicentennial, pointed out that though New Zealanders were 'hungry for useful information about the evolution of their ways of life ... what history could we give them?'. Phillips added that our 'cultural cringe' meant that British history was the focus of university history courses, and undergraduate New Zealand history was not taught until the 1960s. It is interesting to note that the *New Zealand Journal of History* only began in 1967, and the New Zealand Historical Association in 1979. Since the 1993 New Zealand women's suffrage centennial year, there has been a growth in interest in New Zealand women's history.

It is not until critics like Lydia Wevers and Terry Sturm wrote on the subject in the 1980s and the 1990s that a wider ranging assessment of the women writers of the 1945 to 1970 period saw their work as a positive and necessary part of the development of the New Zealand literary canon as a whole. Mary Scott (née Clarke) was born in 1888 and died in 1979. She attended Auckland University College in 1905 to study English, French and History. She graduated MA in English and French, with first-class honours. In the late 1920s Mary Scott decided to start writing, sending articles and stories to magazines and newspapers.

Scott contributed a weekly item to the Dunedin *Evening Star*, for which she was to write for almost 50 years. Wevers writing on Scott states: 'her first two novels, published under the pseudonym Marten Stuart: *Where the apple reddens* in 1934 and the following year *And shadows flee*. These were historical romances set in the far north of early nineteenth century New Zealand' (Wevers, DNZB website). Stevens refers to these two novels as being 'more melodramatic' than her later novels which were published under her own name and were more realistic and humorous, which lifted her novels above the usual label of 'just romance'.

Terry Sturm wrote that Scott was the 'first popular novelist to set all her fiction in New Zealand and to think of her readership as primarily a New Zealand one'. Scott's autobiography, *Days that have been* (1966), and her serious novel, *The unwritten book* (1957), both tell a grimmer story of life in the bush than her popular novels, but all her work stresses the value of bush community and explores the tensions between town and country. She became widely read both in New Zealand and overseas. Many of her books were translated into several languages (like many of the NZ women novelists of the time, for examples see the bibliographical material in the appendices on Eden, Quentin et al) and several became bestsellers in Germany. Scott wrote three collections of plays for country women's institutes, 33 novels, and a monograph under the pen-name J. Fiat.

Included in Scott's novels are five thrillers written with Joyce West (1908–1985). *Fatal Lady* (1960), *Such Nice People* (1962), *Mangrove Murder* (1963), *No Red Herrings*, (1964), and *Who Put it There?* (1965). This is extraordinary in itself, as such collaborations are rare even in producing one book. Stevens has written of West's novel *Sheep Kings* that her material used fresh subject matter 'and she has a keen sense of the drama'. One of West's best-known works is her children's trilogy *Drovers Road* (1953), a tale of family life on a New Zealand sheep station, which was followed by two sequels *Cape Lost* (1963) and *The Golden Country* (1965). West illustrated several of her books with her own ink drawings and contributed poetry and articles to the *New Zealand Railways Magazine*. West's novel *The Sea Islanders* (1970) was turned into a five-part British TV series *Jackanory*.

Nelle Scanlan (1882-1068) worked as a journalist both in New Zealand and overseas. She wrote 15 novels, the most famous of which are the four 'Pencarrow' stories These books established Scanlan as the most popular New Zealand novelist of her generation and in 1963 she published her autobiography, *Road to Pencarrow*, in which she wrote somewhat ruefully: 'I was never young and full of promise. I was once young, but my first novel wasn't published until I was nearly fifty'. Author Alan Mulgan is cited as describing Scanlan as 'a writer who was influential in the 1930s and 1940s in creating a readership for New Zealand fiction, changing negative colonial attitudes towards locally written work'.

The following examples illustrate the extent of women novelists' influence, three of whom are 'Romance' writers, in New Zealand literature in the period 1945 to 1970, both in personal contribution through bibliographical content, and the diversity of their personal lives as an expression of New Zealand life. Each highlights the success of these women writers during the period in either literary or commercial literature, and sometimes both. They appear in chronological order of birth and most have careers extending across the whole period of 1945-1970.

Rosemary Frances Rees: 1876-1963
The cover blurb for Rosemary Rees' 1928 novel *Wild, Wild Heart*, read:

> Miss Rosemary Rees owes her wide popularity in Great Britain and the Colonies to her splendid sense of the open-air life, her understanding of the manly types of manhood and of lovable and unaffected women. She sets the scene of her love stories among natural surroundings, where the promptings of the heart are not checked by convention or pretence. Her men are true men, and her women true women …

Rosemary Frances Rees was the daughter of Hannah (Annie) Elizabeth Staite and William Lee Rees, the youngest of their seven children. Her sister Elizabeth Pococke ('Bessie') Rees (Mrs Hugh Lusk) was also a writer, publishing six novels as 'Elizabeth Milton' between 1929 and 1936. In addition to writing novels, Rosemary

Rees was an actress, theatre producer and playwright. In her entry on Rees for the *Dictionary of New Zealand Biography* Nancy Swarbrick quotes her as saying 'my sole and fervent ambition was to act'. Swarbrick reports that around 1900 Rees went to London to join the company of comedienne Fanny Brough. Subsequently Rees obtained roles with touring repertory companies and wrote short stories for London journals, and several of her one-act plays were staged as curtain raisers.

Rees described herself, as previously suggested somewhat self-disparagingly, as 'the 'best selling' New Zealand author and there is little question of her international reputation as a romance novelist. Patricia Mill, in an interview with Rees in Gisborne in the late 1950s reports that Rees told her that her first novel was 'finished in five-hand-cramping weeks'. Rees explained: 'I wish I could write more solid stuff. I know that my own works are neither profound nor thought-provoking; they are really only very light amusement'. However, Terry Sturm calls her: 'a key transitional figure in the emergence of the light romance in New Zealand ...'

Hyde, who met Rees in 1936, called her likeable and clever, and Rees indicated to Hyde that she knew exactly where she stood and how she was thought of by the literary establishment. Hyde said Rees 'made no bones about writing to sell' ... Rees then told Hyde: 'The Highbrows take themselves much too seriously. Come along and have a cup of tea'. Rees had a lengthy writing career during which she produced 24 romantic novels, and Nancy Swarbrick, writing about these books, explains:

> Some were serialised in major English and American papers before appearing as books, several were published in America (under different titles), and there were numerous reprints and translations. Many had New Zealand settings; this fact and a large local readership established Rees as a key figure in the development of indigenous light romance. The novels were, however, unremarkable: racy dialogue and engaging characters failed to conceal their contrived and predictable plots (Swarbrick, DNZB: 2007).

This, despite the fact that early in her career the 'Boston Transcript' reviewing *Dear Acquaintance* suggested Rees had an emotional gift that the reviewer thought should prove her stepping stone to more lasting literature. Joan Stevens comments of Rees' writings that:

> Nevertheless, such stories have their place in this account of New Zealand fiction. No national literature grows up over night ... the stereotyped characters and the imposed patterns of romance in the novels of Rosemary Rees do not entirely prohibit some good New Zealand touches, and some truthful descriptions of men and things (Stevens, 1966: 43).

J.C. Reid, however, states:

> In the field of popular writing, that demi-monde of letters, women are again to the fore. One of the most popular is Rosemary Rees whose books are only superficially New Zealand novels, for, while she is strong on 'local colour', the values and manners of her characters are English middle-class (Reid, 1946: 57).

Three years before Reid's comment, Alan Mulgan said of Rees that her novels 'did something to break down this indifference [to New Zealand settings]'. It is interesting to note here, that a novel begun in the early 1920s by Ngaio Marsh was set with 'a New Zealand backdrop'.

By the late 1950s Rees was dealing with complex issues in New Zealand's past and her use of local settings had become quite personal also. For example under the heading 'Gisborne romance' the *New Zealand Weekly News* mentions Rees' forthcoming novel *Love in a Lonely Land* as '...set in Gisborne ... [the] story disguises the town in its pioneering era under the name of Gladstone soon after the Te Kooti massacre ...' However, in retirement she was ambivalent: she felt in 'rather a backwater in Poverty Bay - sun and fruit and flowers, but not the stimulation of new ideas'. But a return visit to London in 1957 and celebrity status in the local community provided some compensation. Rees continued to publish novels until about a year before her death, her last being *The Proud Diana* in 1962.

Edith Ngaio Marsh: 1895-1982

Ngaio Marsh was seven years old when her parents moved to Valley Road, Cashmere. The house her father built there was to be her home for the rest of her life. She was educated first at a dame school run by Sibella E. Ross, and then in 1910 enrolled at St Margaret's College, a private Anglican girls' school with an Anglo-Catholic bias, where she remained until 1913, active in literary and dramatic pursuits. Her play *The Moon Princess* was performed that year, with her mother taking the part of the witch. The Christchurch *Press* described it as 'a clever little play', and Marsh herself wrote: 'In the event, it went quite well and drew good audiences', despite some juvenile misgivings.

Between 1913 and 1919 Marsh attended Canterbury College School of Art as a part-time student, supplementing her income with private tutoring. Here she met Evelyn Polson (later Page), who became a lifelong friend, and Olivia Spencer Bower. She shared a studio in Cashel Street with a group of fellow students interested in innovative artistic styles and approaches. The orientation of the college was more formal and academic, but a teacher, Richard Wallwork and his wife Elizabeth, encouraged her. She formed friendships with the Acland family of Mount Peel sheep station and the Rhodes family of Meadowbank sheep station. These associations lasted throughout her life, and were of great importance. The Rhodes appear as the Lampreys in *A surfeit of Lampreys* (1941).

Marsh met Rees after returning to New Zealand from overseas in 1921. Rees had founded a theatre company that Marsh joined, which toured the country with Rees' comic play, *The Mollusc*. Performances were well received in the cities but treated with suspicion in smaller towns, where the view prevailed that 'This Company can't be any good or it wouldn't come here!' After five months Rees was no longer able to pay salaries and, deeply in debt, she abandoned the enterprise. Marsh later described it as 'one of the earliest attempts to found a permanent theatre in this country'.

During this time Marsh was writing articles, poems and stories which were published in the Christchurch *Sun*. She wrote a play, *The Medallion*, which she later regarded as poor though promising. Academic Jane Stafford's DNZB entry on Marsh states that she saw herself as a painter, and in 1927 was included in an exhibition by The Group, organised to differ from the conservative hanging policy of the Canterbury College School of Art. Although she continued to paint, Marsh gave up serious aspirations. She wrote, 'somehow I failed to get on terms with myself'.[17]

In 1928 Marsh travelled to England. Her journey was recorded under her pseudonym 'A New Canterbury Pilgrim', in a series of articles that appeared in the Christchurch *Press* and were syndicated to other newspapers. On her arrival she stayed with the Rhodes family in Buckinghamshire and London. With Nellie Rhodes

---

[17] This is an interesting quote by Marsh concerning herself and may be significant in the chapter on lesbian writers.

she established an interior decorating shop called Touch and Go, in Knightsbridge. She returned to New Zealand in 1932 when her mother became ill.

Before Marsh left Britain she had completed the draft of a detective novel, *A Man Lay Dead*, which she gave to Agatha Christie's literary agent, Edmund Cork of the Hughes Massie agency. He placed it with the publisher Geoffrey Bles, and it came out in 1934. Between 1934 and 1982 Marsh wrote 32 detective stories, shifting to publisher William Collins in 1938, with American publication by Little Brown from 1940. At a time when the detective genre was in the ascendant and predominantly its most admired exponents were women, Marsh became an acknowledged star along with writers Agatha Christie, Margery Allingham and Dorothy Sayers.

Marsh worked within the classic detective story form, enlivening it with the high quality of her writing and a range of erudite references. While many of her novels have an English village or country house setting and subscribe to a conservative view of society, she is capable of innovation, especially in terms of realistic characterisation and psychology. Several works use theatre as a narrative context. Four have New Zealand settings - *Vintage murder* (1937), *Colour scheme* (1943), *Died in the wool* (1944) and *Photo-finish* (1980) - and there are many New Zealand references and characters. Marsh in her long career also wrote works of short fiction as well as some non-fiction and some monographs, articles and essays. She also wrote for theatre, television and radio. Her success as a writer and the financial rewards it brought enabled her to indulge in a taste for expensive designer clothes, often of a strikingly dramatic style. Her theatre directing style was imaginative, meticulous and autocratic, based on her admiration for the theatrical style of London and Stratford.

Despite the amateur status of her actors, the results were highly acclaimed. But she was less sympathetic to any sense of an emergent nationalist culture in her own country, and particularly disliked the New Zealand accent, which she discouraged. This in turn may have lead to a kind of backlash, and she never felt she was recognised as an author in New Zealand. One biographer, Margaret Lewis, pointed out 'The truth is her fiction was admired everywhere in the world except New Zealand'. Lewis commented that Marsh had to keep her more glamorous side concealed because of a New Zealand snobbery about crime fiction. However, critics point to Ngaio Marsh as the first crime writer to bring a novelist's sense of literary style to the genre. She elevated the crime novel to a 'high level of literary art', a *New York Times* review pronounced in 1943. In her autobiography Marsh describes how she began writing detective books in London, on a rainy London day:

> I read a detective novel from a little lending library in Bourne Street. I don't remember the author now, but think perhaps it was Agatha Christie. I was not a heavy reader in the genre but I had, on and off, turned an idea for a crime story over in my mind. It had seemed to me a highly original idea (Marsh, 1966: 216).

Marsh's earlier attempt at a 'New Zealand novel I had laid aside. It was now abandoned for good. I cannot remember what I did with the manuscript' and it seems she began her writing career in the crime story genre almost by accident. She felt that she was never accepted as a real novelist because she wrote detective novels. She was made an OBE in 1948, and a DBE in 1966. She never married, and died on 18 February 1982 at her home in Valley Road.[18]

---

[18] There is further discussion on the life of Ngaio Marsh in the chapter on lesbian writing.

Dorothy Quentin: 1911-1983

Madeleine Murat used 'Dorothy Quentin' as one of her pseudonyms. Others were Martin Tree, Linda Beverly and David King. She was to become a financially successful light romantic novelist, publishing seventy-two books. Little is known of her personal life except that she lived in the UK, Tahiti, and New Zealand (Auckland and Thames) and travelled extensively throughout the world. A note found in the *Weekly News* in 1938 stated:

> Mrs John Batten, whose pen-name is Martin Tree, returned to New Zealand by the Tainui this week. She left the Dominion last November on a flying visit to England. Mrs Batten, who is a cousin to Sir Edward Jerningham, expects to leave New Zealand again, this time to America, where she will accompany her husband to Hollywood (*Weekly News* 9 March 1938: 27).

There are some references to Madeleine Murat in Ian Mackersey's biography of Jean Batten, *Jean Batten: The Garbo of the Skies*, as she was married to the famous aviator's brother, John Batten. Mackersey wrote that John Batten had 'now married the writer Madeleine Murat, and they had a baby daughter Penny, born in August 1933, who, because of the family rift, was never to meet her aunt Jean'. By 1936 the ostracised young family had obviously had enough, and John and Madeleine, 'with their three-year-old daughter Penny, had gone to live in Tahiti where Madeleine continued to write'.

Dorothy Quentin wrote articles for publications other than her own prolific fiction output and the 1948 *Author's & Writer's Who's Who* entry describes her as a 'scenarist'. While her earlier articles and stories remain untraced in *Film Weekly*, in the English women's magazines *Woman's Weekly, Woman's Own, Good Housekeeping* and *Cosmopolitan,* and in the *Australian Women's Weekly*, there is one article that appeared in the English paper *The Mirror* 'What's it really like in London now?' describing life in the English capital during the Blitz. A note with the article says that the author 'returned to New Zealand last February'. Later that year Quentin wrote an article for *The Mirror* that posed the question 'Are war babies wise?'. She answers her own question by advising: 'no, postpone them till the war's end'.

Prior to the war she wrote a regular feature 'Almost in Confidence' in *The Mirror* from June 1938 to December 1939 (and in January 1940 as 'The Round Table') offering advice to readers. The paper introduced Quentin as a married woman, a mother, widely travelled, and someone who has had long experience in dealing with personal problems. These features were often a full page with a chatty note by her on current topics. Later she began to contribute serialised stories to the paper, and a note in 14 Dec.1943 issue of *The Mirror*, with photo, describes Quentin as 'a newcomer among *Mirror* serialists, but an excellent storyteller with a following of millions in Britain and U.S.A.'.[19]

Despite her 'following of millions' Quentin gets only a brief, disparaging mention in the *Oxford Companion to New Zealand Literature* which says her 'romances often read like celebrations of the arrival of American consumerism in the 1950s'. While this may seem somewhat out of fashion, one can imagine many New Zealand women embracing aspects of 'American consumerism' after the many years of deprivation during the depression and war years of the previous decades.

---

[19] My mother was one of those 'millions' who read the romance books by the women writers of the 1950s and 1960s. In fact, they were the only form of literature in our house if you discount my war comics and dad's 'naughty' magazines, a scene played out in households throughout the country at that time, no doubt.

Quentin fares a little better in *The Oxford History of New Zealand Literature in English*. In the chapter on 'Popular Fiction' a page and a half is dedicated to her writing and she gets her own entry in the bibliography section. Sturm writes: 'She was also New Zealand's first author to specialize in hospital romance'. He discusses her novel *Rainbow Valley* (1960), arguing: 'If the plot is flimsy, the celebration of New Zealand is not'. Here Sturm is interested in the eulogizing of American culture by Quentin as he was in the 'Companion'. He quotes Quentin that Auckland is like 'one of those old mediaeval tapestries, full of clear soft colours' ... Queen Street has huge shop windows ... 'bright with beach wear and model frocks and men's sports' wear that shouted of America. Many of the gleaming big cars were American, too'.

Dorothy Eden 1912-1982

Dorothy Enid Eden was born in North Canterbury, on April 3rd 1912, the fourth child of six of John, a mail carrier (earlier a factory hand) and Eva Natalie Eden. Her paternal grandparents were from Gloucestershire and, on her mother's side she was of Danish and Bohemian ancestry. In the introduction to the 1978 edition of *The Vines of Yarrabee* she tells of her mother's parents fleeing the Prussian invasion of Schleswig-Holstein in the 1860s and her father's parents losing all three children on the voyage from England, the last as the ship entered Lyttelton Harbour; four more were born in New Zealand. In her infancy her father began farming in Wakanui, and she grew up on an isolated farm with her four sisters, Marjorie, Winifred, Isobel and Eileen, and a brother Allan, who wrote *Islands of Despair,* an account of his wartime experiences in the sub-Antarctic islands.

Her family was convinced that she should earn a salary with secure employment, and for a while she worked in a Christchurch office, starting work at sixteen as a typist and later as senior clerk for Ashburton lawyer Robert Kennedy. The early stories were published under the name Ena Eden, as she was known in the family. She wrote her first book at the age of twenty and sent several manuscripts to English publishers, one of which was lost at sea during the war, before her first book was published in 1940. She continued to write magazine stories until the late 1970s and several novels were serialised before publication.

She travelled widely and in 1954 settled in London, working for a time in Harrods's bookshop before becoming a full-time writer. She lived for many years in a block of flats in Edwardes Square off Kensington High Street, that locale being transformed into 'Melbury Square' in her novel of that title. Her early books were gothic romances and thrillers and later she also wrote historical novels and family sagas, or 'dynastic novels' as she called them, with settings as diverse as England, New Zealand, China, Ireland, Denmark, Australia, America, and South Africa, with real historical settings such the Chinese Boxer Rebellion and personalities including the love affair in Ireland between Parnell and Kitty O'Shea, all carefully researched.

Eden always wrote by hand, on scraps of paper, during office working hours, during her lunch hour, in bed at night. Then she would type a rough manuscript. Many original hand-written drafts went to Boston University, which established a 'Dorothy Eden Collection' in 1966. By 1980 she was among the ten best-selling authors in the world. Her later books appeared in U.K. and U.S. editions, hardbacks and paperbacks, with Reader's Digest Condensed books, large print and Braille editions, and audio versions.

Her first foreign sale was to her ancestral Denmark, and translations followed into over twenty other languages. Several of her books were broadcast on radio and at least one, *Crow Hollow,* was filmed. Eden's stories appeared over a span of almost fifty years in magazines in several parts of the world (and not just in English) and even when the titles of the magazines are known finding copies to inspect is often difficult. In an interview in *Woman's Choice* (Feb.1956) she talks of writing 'a dozen stories a year', and many were published more than once. A note in *The*

Mirror (July 1960) says that Eden has had her work published in most leading English magazines and in several Continental periodicals, and in one of her articles she is quoted as saying that even she herself had long ago lost count of the number of short stories published in magazines in every English-speaking country.

Eden would sometimes take a temporary position at a job; this provided a change from the hard work of writing thrillers, and 'gives her scope for fresh material. Last Christmas, for instance, she worked for a while in Harrods's book department where she sold the young Prince Charles westerns'. Commenting on her career Eden said in an interview with Peter Isaac:

> It seemed an awfully long time, she says now. One of her remaining ambitions is to have one of her thrillers turned into a film by Hitchcock ... Though there is a strong vein of romance running through Miss Eden's books there is a much more solid core of action ... In spite of her liking for relatively raw action Miss Eden has an intense dislike of ever 'putting a dirty thought in anyone's mind' ... Dorothy Eden, as she admits, writes for people wanting to 'escape, for people who want to dream' (Isaac, 1975: 12-13).

It is interesting to note that after her expression of interest in being filmed by Hitchcock that in an analysis of twenty four best-selling 'modern Gothic' or 'romantic suspense' novels published 1950-1974, focusing on the interrelationships between the male and female characters in terms of their sex-role characterization and the attitudes and behaviour of the hero towards the heroine and the supporting female actor, that Eden is one of the authors analysed. Terry Sturm wrote:

> Gothically tinged mystery and suspense, expertly contrived and resolved, were Eden's trademark ... and in later novels she increasingly drew on the Gothic potential of fairy tales, myths and legends (Sturm, 1998: 158).

Eden returned to New Zealand on a long visit in 1960 at the time of the publication of her New Zealand set novel *Sleep in the Woods*. Never married, she died of cancer on March 4th 1982 and was buried in London. Obituaries appeared in newspapers worldwide. Despite her popularity Eden, like Marsh, has never been regarded as a serious and important writer, although Sturm's writing on her in the OHNZL could be seen as an acknowledgement of her place in New Zealand literature.

Janet Paterson Frame: 1924-2004
Patrick Evans writes:

> The overwhelming sense, as we responded to her death, at the age of 79 on the morning of 29 January 2004, was of a personal loss as with a family member, someone who had lived deep within the warp and weft of our daily lives (Evans, 2004: 15).

In my case this was almost true as Janet's niece, Pamela Gordon, attests, both of us belonging to an extended 'Seacliff' family known as the 'Seacliff Mafia.'[20] Evans

---

[20] Pamela Gordon, Janet Frame's niece, and now her literary executor, wrote an anecdote about me for *The Earl is in ...* a book celebrating 25 years of the Earl of Seacliff Art Workshop (2009). Gordon says: 'But the jewel in the crown concerns the time in the 1990s when we were both living in Seacliff Village and we used to flag the Dunedin-bound Southerner down at the Kilgour Street Crossing and ride that last exhilarating section of seaside track into the city. One day I had a secret rendezvous planned; my aunt Janet

states that he had long been used to his students' insistence, over the years, on referring to her as 'Janet'. He continues:

> in the days after her death I listened to expressions of similar intimacy mingled with the bewilderment of people who clearly did not yet know how to weigh up what they had lost or how they would come to terms with it (Evans, 2004: 15).

Janet Frame was born into a poor Otago family in which there was much personal tragedy and difficulty. Her father worked on the railway and early experiences of poverty and premature death shaped her inner life. The life and work of Frame are well known through her auto-biographical writing and subsequent film by Jane Campion, *An Angel at My Table*, and Michael King's biography *Wrestling with the Angel*, as well as the fact that most of her novels are often assumed to be semi-autobiographical with recognisable friends and family members as the characters. As Evans suggests:

> I began to sense many years ago, when I first sat down and read, in order, everything that she had written: not only that 'the autobiographical' had an unusually intimate relationship to her fiction, but that the two were interchangeable, that, generally speaking, the fiction is where the life is and the life is where the fiction is (Evans, 2004: 15).

This proposition was further confirmed when first Karl Stead and then Frank Sargeson, people who had befriended Frame in Auckland after she left hospital in 1954, also found themselves in print, the former as a young poet in 'The Triumph of Poetry' who sells out to academic life and goes bald, the other as the elderly gay writer in the novel *Daughter Buffalo* (1972). 'It is part of her ... slant on things,' Sargeson complained in a letter to Philip Wilson, 'to collect items about people she knows which she apparently has no second thoughts about using ... it's a sheer bastard when she involves a third party'. But what is interesting about Sargeson, when he 'becomes' Turnlung in *Daughter Buffalo*, is the way Frame seems to give him, with very little sense of artistic transformation, the deaths of her own two sisters as the deaths of his:

> as when she slipped her unwanted brother or her over-attentive Irishman into novels, it is as if she felt able to deal with painful or unpleasant realities through the convention that things in fiction never really happened (Evans, 2004: 15).

What is probably less well known is the number of works published by Frame and about her. My bibliography illustrates the extent of material available by and about her both in New Zealand and overseas. In fact, it is interesting and revealing in the context of this thesis that all the New Zealand women writers in this chapter are, as I have previously stated, rather more well known overseas than in New Zealand, as are some of the poets, for example, Eileen Duggan.

Frame was travelling south from Christchurch and I had arranged to meet her on the train at Seacliff and travel through to Dunedin with her. It was my habit to protect Janet's privacy so I didn't tell Michael [O'Leary] she'd be on the train, but I was delighted when he decided to join me on the journey, just for the hell of it, because it would give me an opportunity to introduce two of my good friends. So here's the story: we got on the train, and when Michael met Janet, he shook her hand and said: "I'm the Earl of Seacliff." She smiled graciously, and said, "And I'm the **Queen** of Seacliff.""

Tara Hawes, in a paper, 'Janet Frame: The Self as Other/Othering the Self', asks 'Why did Janet Frame pretend to be 'of Pacific Island origin' when submitting poems to the *London Magazine* from New Zealand? Later, when she went to England, why did she write from the point of view of 'a West Indian arrival?' The answer comes from Frame herself, and is an example of the playful seriousness of much of her work: 'I wrote a group of poems from the point of view of a West Indian new arrival [in England] and, repeating the experiment that Frank Sargeson and I had made with the *London Magazine* when I pretended to be of Pacific Island origin'. Hawes writes:

> Frame's literature contains many examples of othering the self/selfing the other, such as 'Jan Godfrey' (one of her earliest short stories), where the narrator takes an identity then deconstructs it in the process of the story. The exercise of writing an autobiography is essentially one of othering the self, Frame describing it as an exercise of legitimacy, or making [herself] a first person (Hawes quotes from an interview with Elizabeth Alley, 'In the Same Room', p 40, Hawes, 1995: v.1 n.1).

Firstly then, who is Janet Frame? And who could not be forgiven for thinking that the character, Grace Cleave, in Frame's posthumously published first novel, *Towards Another Summer*, is none other than the author herself, freshly arrived in London for the first time, for example:

> When she came to this country her body had stopped growing, her bones had accepted enough Antipodean deposit to last until her death, her hair that once flamed ginger in the southern sun was fading and dust-coloured in the new hemisphere, and she was thirty, unmarried except for a few adulterous months with an American writer (self-styled) who woke in the morning, said – I write best on an empty stomach, pulled out a piece of paper from his tweed coat hanging on the end of the double bed, and wrote one line. One line every day. She too was a writer, self-styled (Frame, 2007: 11).

Who can this be but the author, and yet … ? The self-deprecating humour is always there, just below the radar, and gives Frame her distinctive New Zealand quality. Hilary Mantel writes in an introduction to the latest edition of Frame's 1961 novel, *Faces in the Water*, that:

> Even more than Virginia Woolf, Janet Frame is the prisoner of her biography; or, to be specific, of the eight years in her life when she was stigmatised as mad, and held in psychiatric hospitals (Mantel in Frame, 2009: vii).

But Frame had already countered what she probably guessed would be said of the book when it was first published. Her disclaimer of autobiography was written in the front of the original edition of *Faces in the Water* and again reprinted in the new edition: 'Although this book is written in documentary form it is a work of fiction. None of the characters, including Istina Mavet, portrays a living person'.

Frame is one of New Zealand's most successful writers. She wrote twelve novels, three volumes of autobiography, five volumes of short stories, two collections of poems, and numerous other short stories and poems published separately. She has also published a work of children's fiction, *Mona Minim and the Smell of the Sun*, and various reviews and critical essays. Mantel commented on Frame's capacity for hard work, stating this debunks the notion of Frame's madness. Mantel makes the point that:

A life so creative, diligent and self-directed suggests not damage or dereliction, but grip and focus beyond the powers of many who have spent a lifetime without their sanity being examined or questioned ... it is a source of exasperation to authors that their work is too often taken autobiographically, and that readers and literary journalists are obsessed with tracking down the 'real-life' places or people behind fiction ... Frame said that in *Faces in the Water* she had softened the truth; she feared that otherwise she would not have been believed (Mantel in Frame, 2009: viii, ix).

The respect in which Frame is held and her popularity as an author is reflected in the many honours and fellowships she has received, including Honourary Doctorates of Literature from the Universities of Otago and Waikato, a C.B.E., and the Turnovsky Prize for Outstanding Achievement in the Arts. In 1990 Frame was awarded New Zealand's highest civil honour when she was made a Member of the Order of New Zealand, and in 2003 she was an inaugural recipient of a Prime Minister's Award for Literary Achievement. Despite all these accolades and awards her work is often hard to find on bookshop shelves outside the main centres in New Zealand. This, according to Frame's literary executor Pamela Gordon, is despite all her novels having been reprinted.[21] Frame died in Dunedin in January 2004.

In highlighting the writing and publishing careers of the five women I have written about in this chapter I make the point that women novelists were neither inconsequential nor insubstantial in the annals of New Zealand literature of the period between the end of WW2 and 1970. However, the women writers presented here appear to have been marginalised and trivialised by much literary criticism of the time. It has only been since publication in the 1990s of Sturm's *Oxford History of New Zealand Literature in English* and Robinson and Wattie's *Companion to New Zealand Literature* that many of these women writers have been acknowledged.

The exception is Frame. She was, however, often seen as an adjunct to Frank Sargeson, and not a threat to male literary dominance because she could be dismissed as being 'mad'. This was the case even up to the later years of her life. For example, when Liverpool writer Linda Grant was asked by Frame's biographer Michael King if she would like to meet Frame during a visit to Dunedin she answered that she would, being an admirer of Frame's work. King, however, warned her of Frame's sensitivity and often reclusive behaviour. Grant wrote:

After forty-five minutes, as instructed [by King], I rose to leave. The next day I flew back to Auckland and ran into a certain level of resentment, that I, a British writer on my first visit to the country, had met New Zealand's greatest living novelist when she was widely believed to be reclusive and a bit mad. She was neither. She simply wanted to get on with writing (Grant, 2009: xvii).

Summing up this chapter on women novelists it is important to note that the majority were far more successful, financially and critically, overseas than in New Zealand and most of them were single. The next chapter discusses three literary and artistic marriages and how the women coped with family life in relation to their literary and artistic ambitions. I include a woman who was a single parent during the period as a point of contrast with the married women.

---

[21] Spotted this staff recommendation at the big Auckland City Whitcoulls branch on the corner of Queen and Victoria Streets: "Janet Frame is one of our most incredible writers. Her works are intense & emotive. A joy to discover".
I'm often asked by visitors to New Zealand why it seems to be so hard to buy Janet Frame's books here in the very country that produced such a great writer on the world stage? It's a good question ... (Gordon, 2009: website).

Chapter 7

Three Marriages and a Single Parent

Some individual examples of marriages of literary women of the period illustrate the issues discussed earlier and show the impact of matrimony on their lives, personal and literary. How did the women in these marriages find time to write as well as doing the work involved in being a wife and mother? In previous chapters I have alluded to the issues of marriage and motherhood, in, for example, the individual case studies of writers in the chapters on women poets and women novelists.

But in this chapter, I specifically analyze three marriages involving couples where both the man and the woman are writers or artists to describe their roles within and without the home. The men are among three of New Zealand's most famous and acclaimed writers and artists - Colin McCahon,[22] James K. Baxter and Alistair Te Ariki Campbell. These three men were married to three talented and independent-minded women: the artist Anne McCahon, poet J.C Sturm[23] (Jacqui Baxter), and poet Meg Campbell respectively.

At the end of the chapter I discuss a poet, Karen Peterson Butterworth, whose individual struggle to become a writer in a solo parent situation contrasts with that of the women of famous male partners. While her individual story takes up the same number of pages as the three marriages together it is important because it covers issues relating to women who attempted to lead independent lives at the time. The fact that Butterworth was not published until many years later proves the point of how difficult it was to become a writer for a woman at that time.

Anne and Colin McCahon

In *Between the lives: partners in art*, a book published in 2005 and edited by Deborah Shepard documenting the marriages and relationships of couples who were prominent in the world of New Zealand arts and literature, Linda Tyler's contribution is titled 'I did not want to be Mrs Colin'. Anne Hamblett was destined to become what she least wanted to be, that is, known as the wife of New Zealand's most famous and respected artist, Colin McCahon. In their early years both McCahons played a large part in the artistic fabric of New Zealand, forming long-term friendships with other artists. In a poem by Colin McCahon written at Titirangi after the McCahons moved from Christchurch he watches his wife Anne and their friend Rita Angus:

> Anne & Rita read each other well,
> Close – so far apart,
> The air between so calm & clear
> With grace and love
> Rita going north,
> Northland,
> Kauri
> (McCahon, 2001: 4).

---

[22] Although mainly known as an artist Colin McCahon wrote a considerable amount of poetry also. In 2001 Peter Simpson edited a collection of poems by McCahon dedicated to his fellow artist Rita Angus who was a friend of Colin and Anne. The book was hand-set and printed by Brendan O'Brien while he stayed for a time at the Rita Angus Cottage in Wellington, and was done in a limited edition of 175 copies to coincide with the Rita Angus Exhibition held at Wellington City Gallery, July-August, 2001.

[23] There is further discussion on the life and work of J.C. Sturm in Chapter 7 on Māori women writers.

According to Dunedin set-designer Rodney Kennedy, Anne McCahon was 'the best artist of her generation' to which Tyler adds that Anne seemed destined to be an artist when she met McCahon, and early in her career Tyler states 'In 1937, however, it was Anne who was the leading Modernist'. Tyler writes:

> However, the demands of marriage, motherhood and making-do on a scanty income from art sales supplemented by poorly paid jobs seem to have exhausted Anne's creativity. While her husband never doubted that he had a contribution to make as a painter, and found supporters for his work, Anne could not sustain her own art-making and recognised eventually that there was room for only one artist in the family. When their son William said in an interview with Agnes Wood [24] in 1992, 'Colin overcame his only real artistic rival by marrying her', he was articulating a situation familiar to many artistic couples where the male artistic [and or literary] genius was dominant and the needs of a creative supportive partner subordinate (Tyler in Shepard, 2005: 31-32).

Gregory O'Brien in his 2007 history of the *New Zealand School Journal* writes:

> Anne McCahon contributed to the Journal regularly over the next eight years [from 1953], producing over fifty illustrations in 1955 alone. With their heavy outlines, the drawings have an affinity with Colin McCahon's early figurative paintings, hinting at a common interest in folk and religious art. Anne McCahon's drawings are impressive for their economy of means, and also – something in short supply amongst New Zealand illustrators at this time – their sense of humour ... While Anne McCahon's career as an exhibiting artist effectively ended in 1945, her drawings are a highlight of the 1950s School Journal and a significant achievement on their own terms (O'Brien, 2007: 119).

Thus we can see the constraints on an acknowledged talented woman artist were such that her own career was literally 'set aside' by family, social and economic constraints and concerns in favour of her husband's artistic advancement.

J.C. Sturm and James K. Baxter

I was a personal friend of both short story writer and poet Jacqui Sturm and poet James K. Baxter, and publisher of Sturm. Theirs was another artistic/literary marriage. Also into this mix of male and female came the added ingredient of their marriage being a bi-cultural one, Māori and Pākehā. While I explore Sturm's career further in Chapter 8 on Māori women writers, it is interesting to note here the successes and ground-breaking aspects of some of her earlier work. Not only was she probably the first Māori woman to obtain a university degree when she completed her BA in 1949, she also was the first Māori writer, male or female, to have a short story published in English in *Te Ao Hou*, in 1954. Throughout the 1940s she had work published in student newspapers and in the 1950s further work appeared in *Te Ao Hou* as well as the literary magazine *numbers*. Paul Millar and Aorewa McLeod state that Sturm's stories:

> are succinct and lucid and on first reading they appear to embrace the era's dominant ethos – that New Zealanders were one nation – by avoiding specific reference to Māori. However, read against the grain of thought that expected,

[24] From MS Papers AG 466, Agnes Wood Collection, Hocken Library Archives and Manuscripts.

in Sturm's words, all Māori 'to become respectable middle-class citizens, a lighter shade of brown, as it were', it becomes clear that the society she depicts fosters inequality, and her work conveys a strong and poignant sense of alienation. Her female narrators, although rarely defined by their race, are marginalized figures that give a vivid sense of the constriction and restrictions of a young woman's life in Wellington in the 1950's (Millar and McLeod, 1998: 518).

In 1948 Jim and Jacqui Baxter (J.C. Sturm) were married and among the many ironies of their life together three points relating to her writing career stand out. Paul Millar writes:

> When her relationship with Jim was commented on, it was almost never acknowledged that she was a writer also. In fact she had begun writing well before she met him, and she has continued writing well after his death (Millar in Shepard, 2005: 140).

Another irony is that she stopped writing poetry soon after they met. In an interview with Millar she confesses that while many people saw Baxter as a drunkard and womaniser:

> Well – he was – But poetry and writing and the whole creative process was what really had captured his life. And as I saw how serious this man was about writing I thought what am I doing, I'm just puddling around. So I stopped (Millar in Shepard, 2005: 147).

In the early 1950s, when Sturm had shifted from writing poetry to writing short stories, they reached a stage where Millar says writing became a companionable adult activity. He quotes Sturm:

> Jim was very supportive of my writing, which was usually done after nine o'clock when the kids were in bed and the nappies were washed (Sturm in Shepard, 2005: 149).

However, by the mid-1950s Baxter's drinking was becoming a real problem for his wife and family. This is reflected in her stories written during this period, but not published until 1983 as *The House of the Talking cat*[25]. Lydia Wevers writes:

> They are narratives of women alone [as opposed to 'man alone'], caring for children, working, and tied to husbands who come home late, drunk unable to offer comfort or protection from the threatening world outside the home. (Wevers, 1998: 284).

Baxter's drinking and his attempts to stop gave rise to a further irony of their marriage. His solution was to seek help by joining Alcoholics Anonymous. But, Millar writes:

---

[25] This collection was republished in 2003 by Steele Roberts, following the successful publications of two poetry collections by the same publisher: *Dedications* in 1996, and *Postscripts* in 2000. Each of these three volumes featured artwork by the Baxter's son, John Baxter.

his new commitment to AA left Jacqui feeling abandoned. Exactly how far apart they had grown became evident when he, without warning, converted to Roman Catholicism. Jacqui was stunned to discover that he could have pursued such an important spiritual path without telling her. The trust that had been shaky for some time evaporated completely. In October 1957 they separated for the first time, a decision Jacqui still regretted four decades later.

Sturm has her own take on events in her poem 'Twenty-five years later':

> In the middle years,
> he patched his coat
> with signs and symbols
> I understood only dimly,
> Chose not to wear too.
> We should not have let them
> separate us as they did
> (Sturm, 2000: 62).

Baxter left home, leaving Sturm with the children and she began working part-time to make ends meet. Baxter had been a School Publications editor between 1956 and 1963 and in the late 1950s he won a Fellowship from UNESCO to study educational publishing in India and Japan. During this trip the family went with him and the couple got back together again. As Sturm states: 'that's where we remarried I suppose you could say. And the children regained their father and family life'. The period through the early and mid-1960s was a stable time for the family, emotionally and financially. But after two years as Burns Fellow Baxter was again feeling stuck. Millar writes:

> He struggled in his marriage, fearing the trap of domesticity; found difficulty relating to his maturing children; and was dogged by the feeling that words had become impotent and should be replaced by actions (Millar in Shepard, 2005: 155).

By the end of 1968 the Baxter family were back in Wellington, but in December of that year Baxter had left to follow his Jerusalem 'vision'. And it was this stage of their marriage that presented perhaps the greatest irony of Sturm's life in relation to Baxter. Millar suggests that the irony lies in the fact that in his final years:

> he came to represent Māoritanga more strongly than Jacqui. His writing records such things as his attempts to learn Māori, the establishment of his tribe of nga mōkai [the fatherless ones] at Hiruharama, and his thoughts on biculturalism. It is an honest record, yet it has obscured the Māori heart at the centre of the Baxter household that had been beating strongly since the 1950s when Jacqui joined Ngāti Poneke and the Māori Women's Welfare League: 'I became pretty involved with the concert party. I went to hui, Māori competitions. And I'd take the children. The children joined ... Jim would come when he could. He'd always sit there very quietly. He was nervous of the whole situation as he hadn't had any experience of it' (Millar and Sturm in Shepard, 2005: 155,156).

In 1969 Baxter was living away from the family and Sturm had effectively become a solo mother again by taking on the task of bringing up her granddaughter. She also became a librarian to earn a living to feed her new family as Baxter had become anti-establishment and anti-materialistic with his new-found philosophy. In

Dedications (1996) Sturm reflects on Baxter's abandonment of her and their family. In the poem 'Grieving, 1972: for Jim' deals with the feelings his actions provoked in her. This is the cry of many women expressing the anger and the grief at being abandoned, either through the breakdown of a marriage or by death of the husband, and in this case both. However, in *Dedications* Sturm also shows how even after so many years and another marriage she still loves him and needs his reassurance. In 'Urgently: for Jim' Sturm writes:

> And bring me safe
> To that bright place
> (I believe –
> I swear I believe)
> Where we may be together
> Again, forever
> (Sturm, 1996: 81).

Sturm's poem also seems to be an answer to Baxter's own poem to her, written in the early 1970s. 'He Waiata mo Te Kare' is a moving and complex poem written to his wife while he was living at Jerusalem, detailing and reflecting on their relationship. In part eight Baxter compares their marriage against the wider aspects of social and personal life.

> I was a gloomy drunk,
> You were a troubled woman,
> Nobody would have given tuppence for our chances,
> Yet our love did not turn to hate.
> ...
> I never wanted another wife
> (Baxter, 1974: 3-4).

Meg and Alistair Campbell
I was a personal friend and publisher of Alistair Te Ariki Campbell and Meg Campbell, another example of literary marriage between two poets. Formerly, Campbell was married to the poet Fleur Adcock, a marriage that did not last. Adcock moved to England where she has received considerable recognition as a poet. While the lives and circumstances of Meg and Alistair Campbell were very different to the Baxters' married life it is interesting to note some similarities in the underlying psychological and spiritual aspects, as written in their poetry to each other, along the lines of Baxter and Sturm. Although the Campbells remained together there were frequent forays by Alistair into other relationships, which he always felt remorse over, but somehow couldn't stop becoming involved in. An expression of this aspect of their lives together is found in a poem from his collection *The Dark Lord of Savaiki*:

> O love, knowing your constancy,
> how did I fail
> to lean it against your heart?
> (A. Campbell, 2005: 89).

Like Baxter's poem it addresses a problem within the relationship and expressed the wish that things could be different. 'I never wanted another wife' says Baxter, although he had effectively left Sturm, and certainly had other women in his life, which is also the case with Alistair in his poem about owning up to an affair. Meg, on the other hand, remains focussed on the fact that despite everything they have remained together. In her poem 'On a Plate: March 2001' she writes about him when he is overseas:

> Our cruelties wear us out, but still
> we remain together.
> Do you understand?
> (M. Campbell, 2005: 37).

'Overlooked and judged unfairly' can be an estimation of Meg's work and life as an 'outside' expression as much as the 'inside' expression found in her own poem. Poet and academic Siobhan Harvey in a recent review of the Campbell's joint 2008 book of poems, *It's Love, Isn't It?* writes that:

> If, in her lifetime, Meg Campbell's poetic gifts were often overlooked, *It's Love, Isn't It?* helps to redress such neglect. Her verse in the book, ably underpinned by a fine introduction from Joy Mackenzie, showcases her as the literary equal of her much-honoured husband ... [her] talent for concision, imagery and expressive language (Harvey, 2009: 107).

Joy Mackenzie, in the introduction to the Campbells' book, writes of the 'likeable personality' behind Meg's poems. Mackenzie continues:

> I admired the way she had survived many trials in her life: marital difficulties, post-natal depression, incarceration in Porirua Hospital, electric shock treatment, marriage to a publicly acclaimed writer, and the difficulties involved in being a second wife and step-mother (Mackenzie, 2008: 7).

Even one of the troubles above would have been enough to cause difficulties in a person's life, let alone a list such as Mackenzie enumerates. Whereas the Sturm–Baxter marriage, for instance, suffered from the changeable nature of their circumstances, financial and personal, the Campbells' situation was unstable in other ways, social and personal, in that Meg was not only seen as 'the woman who broke up a marriage' but that both Campbells suffered from mental illness. As a woman Meg was particularly sensitive to the different treatment meted out to her as a mental health patient. In her essay in *Between the lives* on the Campbells, Mackenzie quotes a 1994 letter she received from Meg. In it Meg writes:

> Alistair's experiences at Porirua Hospital were very different from mine. He was under the care of his good friend Frazer McDonald, and instructions were given not to give him shock treatment because it 'might affect his brain'. Being a well-known figure, I think that Frazer didn't want him tampered with ... it was different for me. I was given several courses, each involving 5X shocks (M. Campbell in Shepard, 2005: 198).

This social/sexual paradigm was prevalent in psychiatric thinking until very recent times. Mackenzie states that:

> Peter Breggin, an American doctor who opposes the use of ECT, has noted that women more often receive electro-convulsive therapy than men because women 'are judged to have less need of their brains'. An investigation into the use of ECT in New Zealand hospitals showed that in 1978 the majority of patients given ECT were women; in one hospital, 75 percent of those receiving ECT were female patients (Mackenzie in Shepard, 2005: 198).

Mackenzie then postulates that Meg is part of a New Zealand literary canon based around women's treatment at the hands of generations of medical practitioners of psychology related illnesses, one of which appears illnesses to be being 'a woman'. Mackenzie states:

> That more women than men endured periods of suffering as psychiatric patients reinforces the need for women writers' accounts of their experiences and treatment, and establishes links in the female tradition. In New Zealand, Janet Frame and Robin Hyde are important forbears (Mackenzie in Shepard, 2005: 198).

From the beginning of their marriage Meg felt she was either 'overlooked or judged unfairly', sometimes both at once. While their love for each other was undoubted, coupled with a shared love for literature, the Campbells' marriage quite quickly became problematic. Meg was guilt-ridden and remorseful about her part in Alistair's divorce from his first wife. She felt out of her depth among Alistair's seemingly sophisticated friends – artists, poets, novelists and editors – and she lost touch with her own friends.

Meg wrote her first poem 'Solitary Confinement' in 1969 while she was in the Female Refractory Ward, Villa 9, Porirua Hospital. By the time I published her book *Resistance* (2005) she had become an accomplished poet. We published 200 copies, the normal small press poetry print-run in New Zealand, which sold out within a short time and I had the feeling that had she been taken seriously as a poet earlier in her career she would be considered as one of New Zealand's best poets.

Karen Peterson Butterworth

In contrast to the trials and constraints of the married women above I now use the example of Karen Butterworth to illustrate some of the difficulties encountered by a solo mother in the 1960s whose ambition to become a writer was thwarted by her circumstances. I have published the poet Karen Peterson Butterworth[26] in my ESAW mini-series (Butterworth, 2006). Butterworth was born on 7th August 1934 in the Catlins, a backblocks district in South Otago. Her father was proud he had finished primary school and obtained his Proficiency Certificate. After he married he was a manual labourer. Her mother had attended high school for one year. Both of them were excellent storytellers. While her mother's chief talent was art, she had two stories and some light verse published in the *New Zealand Listener,* and was a profuse and interesting letter writer, as was her father.

When Butterworth was nine she caught poliomyelitis and was quadriplegic except for her left hand for three months, then gradually regained some strength. For most of the first five months, she could do nothing to pass the time except read. Her father's friends gave her a wooden bookstand to lean against the cradle that covered her legs so that her left hand could turn the pages if the nurses laid her arm beside the bookstand.

Next she started on the school's library books that contained mostly adult classics that had been donated. There were works by Dickens, the Brontés, Charles Reade, Sir Walter Scott, George Eliot, Thackeray, and Hardy. They had gathered dust for decades and her parents had to cut pages for her. Butterworth states:

---

[26] From: 'My Affair With Words' by Karen Peterson Butterworth. This account covers only those life events with a significant impact on her writing and the directions it has taken. Other chapters of her autobiography (still a work in progress) place them in the context of her life as a whole. This work was given to me for use in this thesis by Karen Peterson Butterworth, © January 2010.

I devoured them whole. I was puzzled by the stories of *The Cloister and the Hearth*, *Tess of the D'Urbervilles*, *The Heart of Midlothian*, and *Adam Bede*. My mother had told me that grownups did something that started babies that could only be done within marriage ... I was at a loss as to why Hetty killed her baby and Tess her lover, but concluded that murders must be common in Britain (Butterworth, 2010: unpublished).

Butterworth did secondary school studies by correspondence, and passed School Certificate. She wound down from her exam stress by writing an essay for a competition on the subject 'Our Way to Peace'. She reports:

I'd barely noticed that the prize was a trip to Britain representing New Zealand at the Third World Youth Forum, and my family and I were astonished when I received a telegram saying I was one of five finalists, and could I please come to Wellington for an interview? Mum and I travelled to Wellington by slow train, boat train express and Lyttelton ferry, a great adventure for me (Butterworth, 2010: unpublished).

During that year Butterworth's English teacher announced that an Otago woman writer had won a famous short story prize. Her name was Janet Frame. She bought copies of Frame's book for the class and they all read it. Butterworth reports:

It was a revelation to me that writing about everyday Otago life was legitimate – my reading until then had all been set in Britain or Europe. Only at 'varsity did I discover other New Zealand writers including Katherine Mansfield, Frank Sargeson, and Robin Hyde (Butterworth, 2010: unpublished).

Butterworth thought the best way to obtain further training in writing was to do a four-year journalism cadetship. But the Vocational Guidance Officer said flatly, 'No. With your polio you couldn't carry a heavy typewriter about with you to assignments'. She turned down her next six career choices too, on the grounds they were too heavy physically (e.g. horticulture) or women didn't do them (law). She suggested library work, in which Butterworth had no interest. But she got a part-time job at the university library to pay for her studies and living costs and began to study part-time for her arts degree, majoring in English.

She saw an advertisement for a cadet at the *Taranaki Daily News* and answered it. She was successful, with three years taken off the cadetship for her English units, meaning she could qualify as a junior journalist after only one year. However, on her first day at work, the editor called her into his office and said something like: 'I don't hold with women reporters, but the Board forced my hand. You can't gather news in pubs, and I have to pay you a full wage'. The Journalists' Award was one of the few without a separate lower rate for women, who were so rare the negotiators never thought of them. However, respectable women couldn't go into public bars, where the best news was to be found. Butterworth explains:

I left his office fuming. Then I was called into the Chief Reporter's office. George Koea, who was later married to novelist Shonagh Koea, was my immediate boss. He said something like, 'Don't listen to that old fogey. It was my idea to hire you, and I look forward to our association.' At twenty-five he was the youngest Chief Reporter in the country, and one of the best. I promptly fell in love with him, but a relationship between boss and a worker of the opposite gender was unthinkable then. I'm sure he never thought of it (Butterworth, 2010: unpublished).

Also on the staff was Harry Dansey, cartoonist and Illustrations editor. He and George taught her a great deal about Māoritanga, of which as a South Islander she explains she was largely ignorant. The *Taranaki Herald*, the local evening paper, would not employ Māori. The *Daily News* was exceptional in Taranaki, where everyone, Māori and Pākehā alike, carried a load of historical racial grudges. Butterworth says that George Koea gave her wonderful basic training.

He made Butterworth second-string drama critic, and frequently called her to his office for long chats on artistic subjects. However, she says that his close proximity and her hopeless love for him caused her so much agony that after a year, when she had qualified as a J1, she left to become a publicity officer in an overseas aid organization in Wellington. She was then on female wages from 1957 until 1967 when she joined the Public Service which by then had equal pay.

One day Butterworth climbed the stairs to the Teachers' College library, where by the late 1960s she was training to be a teacher, with an armful of books and fainted at the top. Before she was fully conscious the staff asked if she was pregnant and she said 'yes'. College rules at that time meant she had to leave immediately, but could apply for re-admission a year later. Her landlady heard and evicted her, and she was suddenly without an income or a place to stay. Her thoughts were at the time:

> Here was rich material for writing, and in the absence of study obligations words began to flow in my evenings alone with my Smith Corona and a one-bar heater. I wrote a short story ('Johnny's Paalagi') and several anguished self-indulgent poems, none of which was ever published (Butterworth, 2010: unpublished).

No employer at the time would employ visibly pregnant single girls. By five months her pregnancy was showing and it seemed as if a home for unmarried mothers was Butterworth's only option. She could not go back to her parents, who lived in a small community and would never be allowed to forget her 'shame', especially considering that the child's father was a Samoan.

It was not easy and she was too busy and tired to write much for eighteen years. However, she drafted a novel about two single girls sharing a state house and bringing up their babies. It was to be a satire about overcoming government and teachers' college bureaucracies. Meanwhile she kept attending College though she found it difficult. She had been corresponding with a Māori man who had a dairy farm and wanted her to marry him. She states:

> he wrote poetry in Māori and English. He was of rangatira descent and had been educated at St Stephen's College ... I married [him] mainly to relieve my stress level. I soon realised my husband was mentally unwell ... he would show no-one his art or poetry, and having shown them to me became suspicious that I would reveal them to others. The end came soon after he claimed I was trying to poison him ... one day when I tried to get through to him, he responded by beating me up ... He said he was going to a hui, and I and the tamaiti must leave before he came home, as he didn't trust himself ... the kaumātua of his hapū were very supportive (Butterworth, 2010: unpublished).

She left her son with her parents (who passed him off as her stepson to avert gossip) for a few weeks while she arranged to go back to teaching and find accommodation. Butterworth found a Probationary Assistant's position in Lower Hutt and rented a bach in a couple's backyard.

At that time there were only widows' and deserted wives' benefits. Single mothers and divorcees obtained what they could through the courts, provided they could afford a lawyer. Single mothers were entitled to maintenance for their children only, while separated or divorced women could also sue for their own maintenance. A group organized a delegation to see a senior manager in the Department of Social Welfare, who told them there was a widows' and deserted wives' benefit, and there wasn't one for men, because research showed children were best off living with their mothers.

They soon had the chance to make submissions to a Royal Commission on Social Security. Butterworth wrote their submission and testified before the Commission. After Parliament had received the Commission's report it legislated for a number of reforms, among them the Domestic Purposes Benefit. She felt they shared the credit for this with the many church organisations who had testified similarly. She states:

> Some people snubbed me for the 'shame' of my situation, which in their eyes was exacerbated by my child's racial mixture. (There were at that time also many people who stigmatised divorced and separated women) ... friends and relatives kept pestering me to give up my son for adoption and/or look for a husband. I responded by saying, 'one day, I'll get married'. This was exactly what happened when my son was eleven. The social support I received from my immediate family (by letter), the Society of Friends which I attended, and my fellow solo parents, kept me from sliding into depression (Butterworth, 2010: unpublished).

Butterworth found a part-time editing job in the Department of Education. She began saving for a deposit on a state house. She remained in the basic grade for three years, with annual rises within its scale. During this time she also finished her degree part-time. In 1968 her job came under threat in a recession. Part-time workers could be sacked without notice, so she negotiated to work full-time and organized good child-care for her son.

Butterworth became active in the Public Service Association, serving successively on the Women's, the Part-time Work, and the Child Care subcommittees of its Executive Committee. If you wanted to move up a grade, you needed to apply for higher positions. She rose from Grade I to Grade XI but after failing six interviews, she suspected she was blacklisted for her union and political activities.

Not until the early 1990s was Butterworth at last able to write seriously. She has since published a book of her local newspaper columns and two poetry collections, edited or co-edited five non-fiction books and a haiku anthology, won prizes and been published in literary magazines and anthologies in seven countries including New Zealand. In Māori Language year she commenced seven years of part-time study of Te Reo Māori, two of them at Te Wananga o Raukawa, and wrote some poems in te reo, winning the Whitireia Poetry Competition Award.

In this chapter I have included all this detail in order to illustrate the dynamics in the lives of women who wanted to become writers and artists and the constraints and difficulties, personal, economic and societal that affected their careers. Both in statistical and individual instances I have provided evidence of the variety of reasons why women writers experienced constraints on their careers, whether these were family commitments, low self-esteem, lack of support from friends or society generally, the fact that their husband's careers took 'centre stage' even though that often underscored the instability which the marriages suffered because of their husband's often erratic employment, while Butterworth's story is an example of the struggle of a solo parent, both political and personal.

In the following chapter on Māori women writers the discussion centres around what could be termed a 'non-existent' literary tradition if looked at from the literary norms at the time. Added to sex discrimination, the factors of race were an additional constraint in the New Zealand of the period.

Chapter 8

Māori Women Writers

In this chapter I discuss the Māori women writers and their virtual non-existence in the New Zealand literary world before the 1970s, when Patricia Grace of Ngāti Raukawa, Ngāti Toa and Te Āti Awa published her first work, *Waiariki*, said to be 'the first book of stories written by a Māori woman' (O'Brien, 2007: 71). Until the late 1960s and the early 1970s Māori writers in New Zealand were scarcely mentioned in the annals of New Zealand's national literature. The names of Hone Tuwhare, Ngā Puhi, Witi Ihimaera, Te Aitanga-a-Māhaki, Ngāti Porou, and Rore Hapipi (Rowley Habib), Ngāti Tūwharetoa, are the more obvious male writers who began to be noticed. However, there were also Māori women writing during the 1940s to the 1970s period, none of whom appeared in the major poetry anthologies of the time.

No Māori woman, no cry

Neither Curnow's *A Book of New Zealand Verse*, (1945) nor *An Anthology of New Zealand Verse* (1956) edited by Robert Chapman and Bennett, included any Māori women poets. Some Māori women writing at the time may have been composers of waiata, powhiri, and other traditional forms of verbal expression, and although their works may not have reached beyond the Marae and the local tribal areas where they were written and performed during this period, they should have been acknowledged in these major anthologies as weavers of the word in Aotearoa New Zealand.

Erihapeti Murchie

One composer of waiata and poetry is Erihapeti Murchie, a rangatira me wahine toa of Kai Tahu, Kati Mamoe, Waitaha and Ngāti Raukawa. Born and raised at Arowhenua, near Temuka, her work encapsulates the definition given above and she is a good example of a Māori woman who wrote about living in the Pākehā world and Te Ao Māori, and who had achievements in both, beyond most people's ability to succeed in only one. While at Christchurch Teachers' College Erihapeti met and married Malcolm Murchie, a Pākehā from Whanganui. Together they had ten children and both shared a common interest in politics, the arts, conservation and social justice, attending rallies against apartheid in South Africa and the Vietnam War. In an unpublished memoir titled 'What I Believe' Erihapeti stated:

> My attitudes and my hierarchy of beliefs have filtered through from the ancestral past of a largely dispossessed takatā whenua (people of the land – the Māori) ... my people will retain their status as kaitiaki ö te mauri ö te whenua (custodians of the spirit of the land) ... shaping of a culture distinctly Aotearoa New Zealand that blends Polynesian with other European elements (Murchie, private papers: unpublished).

Along with her Ratana religious beliefs these kaupapa underpin Erihapeti Murchie's life. She did much to help her people both formally and informally. When her family moved to Dunedin she was instrumental in obtaining the site for the urban marae, Araiteuru, and her whānau would awhi many young Māori students living in the predominantly Pākehā city of Dunedin in the 1960s and 1970s. Among her many official positions she was National President of the Māori Women's Welfare League, 1977 to 1980. During this period she completed a Māori research project, Rapuora Health and Māori women, and she was active in getting government policies changed in Māori health, te reo Māori, and education. In 1989 Victoria University conferred on her an Honorary Doctorate in Law.

Coupled with these outward achievements, Erihapeti Murchie also composed and taught waiata to her whānau to ensure they understood and remembered their ancestral links to Kai Tahu and Kati Mamoe. When she died in 1997 the Kai Tahu whakatauki 'Whaia ki te tei tei' (reach for the highest peak) was given to her whānau in recognition of her achievements. One of Erihapeti Murchie's waiata shows her talent for composition on the spot. At the tangi of Kai Tahu leader Tipene O'Regan's father there was no song for his poroporoaki so she was able to sing this waiata atāhua, 'Papaki te Tai', which she composed spontaneously:

Papaki te tai ki uta ra
Whatiwhati te waka, tere iho ki raro ra,

Tumokemoke te iwi ki raro e,
Te korowai o te Aitua, o kaa roimata e,

Takihia mihia poroporoaketia
Haere hoki e te wairua ki kaa tupuna e

Waihoa matou hei whakawhiriwhiri
Te ara tika mo kaa mokopuna
I tēnei Ao hurihuri e

'Waves crashing'

Waves crashing against the cliff,
The waka is broken down below,

The iwi sit in sadness under,
The cloak of the Aitua, and tears

We've wept, mihied,
The spirit has returned to the tipuna,

And we will remain to seek
The right path of the mokopuna
Within the changing and turning world
(Murchie, private papers: unpublished).

A poem, 'Awarua (Te Hura Kohatu)', written at Arowhenua sees Murchie in a reflective mood, thinking about the impermanence of life and her interpretation of and affinity with nature:

I have a passion here
For quiet waters brooding deep
In the curve and sweep of a narrow trough meandering
Through willowed banks,

And languid in its flow
The white dressed cress is haunt
To the water crabs and speckled trout
That taunt the dragon flies
Skimming the stream
And slim black eels within,

Aloft in trembling flight
The flick flack tiwaiwaka
Pirouetting its delicate haka
And the Little White Bridge
Triumphant stands still
To spring floods,

But life is ever changing
With voices stilled and the richness
That the tidal flow is witness to
Has ebbed – and Awarua
No more chatters
Free from the bridge below.
(Murchie, private papers: unpublished).

Māori researcher, historian, and composer of waiata, Charles Royal, has written about the aspect of Moteatea that Murchie evokes so well. Whilst Royal is talking generally about the art form in an historical context his words could equally apply to her writing. Royal writes:

Clearly Māori did and do create poetical compositions which might be described as literature, particularly oral literature; yet the term fails to capture the entirety of the tradition. For example, most writers in the West have since the Renaissance intended their works to be represented on the written page. Moteatea [Māori song or poetic composition] composers on the other hand conceive their work essentially for performance, while the 'literary' quality of the texts cannot be denied (Royal, 1998: 346).

Maewa Kaihau

Another example of a Māori woman writing, this time early in the 20th Century, is Maewa Kaihau, who wrote the words to the tune *Now is the Hour* which began as a modified Swiss lullaby for the singing of *Po Atarau* to farewell Māori World War One soldiers. In 1920 Kaihau wrote a *This is the Hour* verse, and in 1935 she again adapted the *Po Atarau* verse. This became the *Haere Ra Waltz Song*, which was sung when steamships were departing New Zealand for overseas. English wartime singer Gracie Fields learnt *Haere Ra* on a visit to New Zealand in 1945. Her version of it, known as *Now is the Hour*, became a world-wide hit in 1948. The first and last verses became extremely popular, and Kaihau claimed that all the words and tune were her own work.

Kaihau's words were not copyrighted until 1928 and more recently Dick Grace has claimed most of the words as the work of his family. In those days before radio and before locally-made recordings, the lyrics of this song were probably being changed constantly according to circumstance and memory, and Kaihau's genius was to mold a version whose words could be understood and appreciated by both the Māori and Pākehā communities:

Perhaps the chief factor contributing to the success of *Now is the Hour* as a representative New Zealand song is its reflection of the Māori/English amalgamation fundamental to the national fabric (Annabell, folksong.org: 2007).

Te Ao Hou

For the Māori women writers who did make it into the print medium in the 1960s, including Grace, their main vehicle for publication during the period covered by this thesis was the Māori Affairs Department magazine, *Te Ao Hou*. Were it not for *Te Ao Hou* and the *New Zealand School Journal* many Māori women writers would conceivably not have entered into 'the world of light' at all. In an early 1970s edition of the magazine an article 'The Māori Contribution to New Zealand Literature' states:

> Māori poetry is distinguished from prose by: —
> (a) the fact that it is fixed-form — once the composition has been set in its frame and polished by the author, it is repeated word for word in song form, subject occasionally to slight modifications (a word is changed or a line is dropped), due to errors of memory or dialectical differences.
> (b) by its manner of delivery, which is essentially musical.
> (c) by certain distinctive stylistic features such as the stylisation of metaphor, symbolism, allusion and ellipsis.
> Māori poems abound in these, be they dirge, lament, lullaby, ditty, love song or derisive song. They all breathe the spirit of place, evoke the very clap of thunder, flash of lightning, lash of wind and rain, caress of zephyr, moon and sun, pungent sense of environment and climate, intimacy in the colour and drama of landscape. Although there are some fine translations of Māori song poetry, ritual chants, watch alarms, etc, they do not always capture the rhythms of speech, the undulations of melody, the music of words that soothe the ear, move the mind, rouse the spirit and stir the imagination (Anon, *Te Ao Hou* 1973 No. 71: 36, 37).

The article points out that a further distinction between poetry and prose is its manner of delivery, which is essentially musical. Karakia, canoe-launching chants, poi chants, and laments were often composed and performed by women. A good example is Tangikuku's lament in which she likens herself to a cicada that is short-lived and very soon to die. She was a poetess who was so emaciated by asthma that she could not join a party of women on their way to the rocks to dive for crayfish and gather sea-eggs and paua, thus her lament. The article went on to state that the classic chant 'Piki mai, kake mai' was a tribute to writers who 'bring light' into the world and suggested:

> Overseas scholars who have studied Māori oral literature are astounded by the variety of literary forms and devices, by the depth of speculative thought, the vividness of imagery, the wealth of cultural allusions, and the rhythm of tragic and beautiful phrases (Anon, *Te Ao Hou* 1973 No. 71: 36, 37).

Arapera Blank
Among the Māori women writers of the time between 1945 and 1970 two stand out as having a literary profile in the general literary world. Arapera Blank and J.C. Sturm were both published authors as well as regular contributors to *Te Ao Hou*. For example, Arapera Blank won the prize for the best short article in the Katherine Mansfield Memorial Competition for 1959.

Her article described kumara growing in her district, the isolated northern area of Rangitukia. It was published in *Te Ao Hou* in October 1958, and was her first attempt at writing. The distinction of winning a Mansfield Memorial Award was considerable. Maurice Duggan won the short story award, and Elsie Locke the non-fiction one. The sponsors (the N.Z. Women Writers Association and the Bank of New Zealand) decided to add two further awards, one for the best short article, won by Arapera Blank. The official announcement read as follows:

> Another excellent entry was placed top in the short article division. Mrs Arapera Blank had been placed top of the shorter articles for her entry *Ko*

Taku Kumara Hei Wai-U Mo Tama in the Māori Affairs Department publication *Te Ao Hou*. Her article was written in English. Mrs Blank is a Māori writer and a teacher at Punaruku. Her work has developed through the opportunities given to Māori writers through *Te Ao Hou*. It is arresting and creative. For the excellence of the above two entries (the other was by O. E. Middleton) the Bank of New Zealand decided to make additional prizes of fifteen guineas each ... (Anon, *Te Ao Hou* December 1959, No. 29: 4).

J.C. Sturm

Jacqueline Cecilia Sturm (J.C. Sturm: **Taranaki, Whakatohea)**, was born in Opunake in 1927 and is a writer of short stories and poetry. In the late 1940s her poetry was published in student newspapers and the *Otago University* Review. As discussed in the previous chapter she married the poet James K. Baxter in 1948. In 1950 she began an MA in Philosophy at Victoria University, writing a dissertation on 'New Zealand National Character as Exemplified in Three New Zealand Novelists', which was commended as being of exceptional merit and awarded first class honours.

Sturm's story 'For All the Saints' became the first story written in English by a **Māori** writer to appear in *Te Ao Hou*. Throughout the 1950s and early 1960s she featured regularly in *Te Ao Hou*, both writing and reviewing. Editor C.K. Stead included Sturm's story 'For All the Saints' in *New Zealand Short Stories: Second Series*, making her the first **Māori** writer selected for a New Zealand anthology.

Early in the 1950s she began writing short fiction: in 1954 her first story 'The Old Coat' appeared in the first issue of the quartley literary magazine *numbers* and in subsequent issues until it finished in 1959. Aorewa McLeod and Paul Millar in their entry for *The Oxford Companion to New Zealand Literature* say of Sturm's work that the stories are succinct and lucid and on first reading they appear to embrace the era's dominant ethos, which was that New Zealanders were one nation, by avoiding specific reference to **Māori**. However, they continue, reading against the grain of thought that expected all **Māori** to become respectable middle-class citizens, in other words a lighter shade of brown, and it becomes clear that the society she depicts fosters inequality, and her work conveys a strong and poignant sense of alienation.

According to McLeod and Millar, J.C. Sturm's female narrators, although rarely defined by their race, are marginalised figures that give a vivid sense of the constriction and constraints of a young woman's life in Wellington in the 1950s. They quote Lydia Wevers who notes that by supplying 'the missing term 'Māori' Sturm's stories fall horrifyingly into place'. Sturm herself commented that 'whether my work has any [overt] Māori content or not we're talking about a way of looking, a way of feeling and a way of being'.

By 1966 Sturm had a collection of stories ready for publication, but no publisher. In 1969 she became a solo parent and the pressures of earning a living left her little time for further writing for over 20 years. In 1982 two stories, 'First Native and Pink Pig' and 'Jerusalem, Jerusalem', were featured in the anthology of **Māori** writing Into the *World of Light* co-edited by Witi Ihimaera. Then the women's publishing collective Spiral printed her stories in 1983 as *The House of the Talking Cat* which was shortlisted in the New Zealand Book Awards. In a 1984 article Ihimaera called her a 'pivotal presence in the Māori literary tradition' and speculated on the course Māori literature might have taken had 'J.C. Sturm and Cat achieved success and publication in their time, rather than twenty years later'.

In the decade following the publication of *The House of the Talking Cat* Sturm returned to writing poetry. Through her experiences of loss and love, youth and age, and Māori and Pākehā, Sturm's verse conveys a sense of tranquillity and acceptance of the dualities inherent in her own eventful life. In 2003 she received an honorary Doctor of Literature degree from the Victoria University of Wellington. J.C.

Sturm's place in the sociological and psychological context of the period and the remarkable achievement of her writing and life as a contribution to the present generation of Māori women and her insight about how Aotearoa New Zealand is developing is expressed in an article she wrote for *Te Ao Hou* in 1954:

> When I was preparing this article, some one asked me why are the Māori WOMEN in the vanguard of welfare work? Does this imply that the status of women in the Māori community at large has changed, giving them more say in all matters Māori? Frankly, I do not know. But I would suggest that nearly all the disadvantages of the Maoris' position are felt most acutely in the home, so that it is the women, not the men, who have to cope with them daily, understand them more fully, and are most strongly moved to do something about them. If the explanation is more complex than this, if the Māori women today really have more vigour and initiative than the men, well, good luck to them! (Sturm, *Te Ao Hou* No. 9, Spring, 1954: 8).

A recent visual biography has been made of Sturm's life titled, 'Broken Journey: The Life and Art of J.C. Sturm'.[27] At the time aged 80, Stum reflects on her life and the influences that shaped her writing, including her early years in the Taranaki coastal town of Opunake, as well as the impact of her local pā, Parihaka. The title refers to her 'broken' writing career as she had to attend to family matters from the late 1960s to the late 1980s, first being a deserted wife and then a widow, as well as bringing up her granddaughter from-infancy, and working as a librarian.

In her later years J.C. Sturm has become a renowned kaituhi (poet) in her own right. The film's director, Tim Rose, says the hour-long documentary is an intimate story of a long, well-lived life. As she tells the story of her life, a narration in the Māori language paints the picture of parallel events in New Zealand society – the depression and the war, urbanisation, the changing role of Māori women, and Māori women in literature. Originally, she makes the point in the film, in the 1950s and 1960s she felt she was 'not a poet' as she thought she was not in the same league as her famous husband and his literary friends.

Another consideration as to why Sturm switched from poetry to prose, as she did at this time in the 1960s, could be due to a prevailing idea that men could write poetry and women couldn't. For example, one of her husband's colleagues, Louis Johnson, with whom Baxter co-edited the literary quarterly *numbers* stated:

> Since we've been asked to look at the problem in this battle-of-the-sexes way, we might generalise that our women contributors appear to be more proficient at prose than with poetry (Johnson, 1957: 28).

Sturm reports that she would show her husband poetry she had written and he would simply say nothing, neither good nor bad. While this may have been his way of not wanting to appear biased, she found this a most disconcerting experience.

Rose, from the Paekakariki-based Kapiti Productions, whose parents lived next door to the Baxter whānau in Wellington, reports that he knew Jacqui:

> pretty much since the day I was born. I have spent time with Jacqui in the last couple of months [while making the film] talking with her about her life and the things that have influenced her writing. The more time I spend, the more the stories flow. At times very personal, they weave from home and family to literary history and culture in an ever changing story. It's a jigsaw of treasures,

[27] 'Broken Journey' screened for the first time on Māori Television's New Zealand Documentary slot, Pakipumeka Aotearoa, on Wednesday October 17, 2007.

each piece essential to the other and in total, the key to national knowledge and collection
(Rose,www.throng.co.NewZealand/documentary/broken-journey-the-life-and-art-of-jc-sturm:website).

J.C. Sturm died on the 30th of December 2009, her tangi was held on her home marae near Opunake and later she was farewelled in a moving ceremony and celebration at Paekakariki, the seaside village on the Kapiti Coast where she lived much of her adult life. In an obituary by fellow poet Jeffrey Paparoa Holman, he called her 'a pioneering literary figure'. Holman continued:

> Her Māoriness became a very private thing to her and still is ... Baxter's sudden and precocious appearance in New Zealand's literary firmament in the 1940s overshadowed much of her adult life. Moving among the male-dominated literary circles of a vigorous Wellington artistic community during the 1950s and early 1960s, Sturm found an editorial champion outside of Pākehā gatekeepers who could not conceive of a Māori literary tradition: Erik Schwimmer [who] managed to persuade the conservative Māori Affairs department to fund a journal of Māori writing, by Māori, for Māori, *Te Ao Hou*, which he then edited. Seeking out Sturm, he asked her for a story ... Sturm's late-blooming literary career began in earnest, and when she turned again to writing poetry in the 1990s, her real talent in forms other than prose fiction was apparent ... like many women writers of her generation, [she] had to sacrifice their gifts and abilities on the altar of domesticity. In her case, she had also to carry the burden of being a Māori woman in her generation (Holman, *Dominion Post* 11-1-2010).

We may conclude that the development of Māori writing would have been greatly enhanced if this talented writer had been able to publish her work during an earlier period.

Tuini Ngawai

The following excerpt from an editorial in the April 1956 issue of *Te Ao Hou* indicates how highly literary prowess was held in Māoridom, but also shows how little was known of the flourishing Māori literary scene in the wider literary world, and the fact that many writers and poets were women, as demonstrated by this article about Tuini Ngawai:

> The publication in this issue of the winners of our first successful literary competition is a landmark for *Te Ao Hou* ... There have been Māori writers since the alphabet was introduced. Many of the beautiful stories published in Sir George Grey's *Ngā Mahi a Ngā Tupuna* were originally written by Māori historians ... Fine examples of Māori writing are found in magazines like *Te Waka Māori, Te Hokioi, Te Wananga, Te Pipiwharauroa, Toa Takitini, The Polynesian Journal*, and so forth. Much of the best writing by Māoris today is in English ... [however] the preservation of the Māori tongue depends on its continued use for literary purposes, as in song and oratory. As there are only a limited number of people who reach a high standard in literary Māori, they do a great service by publishing their work so that their example can be more widely followed ... writing is a very important activity and Māori writers do a great service to their race. Most Māoris think a good deal about their people and the things that affect them. To a great extent, the future of the people depends on how good that thinking is ... [they] may describe how a meeting-house was built, or how the old people used to live, or what it feels like to live in a town, or

to own a taxi business ... The subjects need not be practical. Family life, love and death, have been subjects for writers and poets from time immemorial.[28] People like to tell stories and people like to listen to them (Anon, *Te Ao Hou* No. 14, April 1956: 1).

Tuini Ngawai was descended from Te Whānau-a-Ruataupare ō Ngāti Porou. Her teaching career ended in 1946, when she took on the leadership of shearing gangs. Ngawai expected strict standards from her workers, and won the women's section of a shearing competition. Many of her songs commemorating Māori shearing gangs are still sung on the East Coast. From 1946 she also became involved with the Kotahitanga movement, which sought to restore Māori pride and identity through cultural revival. She assisted the tohunga Hori Gage in his healing ministry, and she was involved with efforts to achieve greater recognition for the Treaty of Waitangi.

Ngawai voiced her deepest feelings through the words of songs such as 'Te Kotahitanga ra e' and from the mid 1940s to 1963 Tuini put to use her versatility with a number of instruments, especially the saxophone, by leading a six-piece band she named the ATU Orchestra. Most of her songs were set to popular tunes because, for Ngawai, their vital message lay in the words rather than the music, and the performers had to learn the songs by heart as quickly as possible for each new occasion. From 1953 Ngawai entered her senior cultural group from Te Hokowhitu-a-Tu in the Tamararo Māori cultural competitions held in Gisborne.

Ngawai trained and entered two youth groups and most years these three groups represented Tokomaru Bay in the annual competitions. She wrote many songs for these events, including 'Piki mai kake mai', to commemorate the ancestor for whom the competitions were named. Ngawai and Te Hokowhitu-a-Tu sang her song 'Te Tiriti o Waitangi' before Queen Elizabeth II during her tour of 1953–54. Another famous song of the 1950s was 'Nau mai, haere mai', written to welcome the 1956 South African rugby team to Gisborne. Anaru Takurua writes of Tuini:

> She was a perfectionist with an unrelentingly high standard, although she allowed for individual style and did not insist on a rote-learned unison in cultural performances. Although a Ringatu she assisted other churches with their choirs, in combined worship and in Māori cultural activities. Her greatest contribution to other churches was in leading a Mihinare (Anglican) culture group at the all-Aotearoa Hui Topu Māori held at Turangawaewae marae in 1962. For this occasion she wrote 'Matariki', one of two songs she penned to acknowledge her King movement hosts (Takurua, DNZB website: 2007).

In the *Te Ao Hou* No. 14 issue there was an article on her as a poet/songwriter Ngawai:

> The first person I met on Makomako station was the manager. He seemed rather surprised to hear that to-day's leading Māori songwriter was at that moment working in his shearing shed, but at the name 'Tuini Ngawai' he showed recognition. Yes, she was there. But, he added, to see her in the shed, you wouldn't believe she had composed any songs (Anon, *Te Ao Hou* No. 14, April 1956: 46).

---

[28] It is interesting to note that 'family life, love and death' are not considered by the editor to be 'practical' subjects. It is highly likely that this particular editor is a man rather than a woman for in the Māori world, and many other worlds, these three things are definitely 'practical' things to be taken care of by the women in that particular society.

81

The author of this piece in *Te Ao Hou* is an unnamed Pākehā writer who wanted to translate her songs and is overwhelmed by this Māori song-writer whom he finds has 'a consciousness of the hidden depths of the mind that is in general more typical of writers than shearers.'

This did not surprise me, however, as I have worked on many labouring jobs. Whether it was laying tracks on the railway or digging drains I often found more kindred 'poetic spirits' among labourers, particularly Māori and Polynesian and those of Irish descent, than I encountered in the 'career conscious' atmosphere of university or intellectual circles. The *Te Ao Hou* article noted that like many poets, Ngawai has had words dictated to her by something outside her consciousness, 'in a dream,' she says.

For example, *Arohaina Mai* which she regards as her best song, took only a few minutes to compose but like many writers the words come from subconscious thinking over many years and experiences; like the English Romantic poet William Wordsworth's definition of poetry, 'experience reflected in tranquillity'. And the politics behind much of Ngawai's works are clear. The Māori people, she said, were still wonderful singers, but actions for the songs were often poor due to the words not being understood fully or even at all. She thought that teaching action songs in schools would be unrewarding unless the language was also taught. Ngawai said that she liked the shearing routine and liked to live for a while with young people and to keep in touch with how they felt. The author finished his *Te Ao Hou* article in a pertinent fashion:

> After my visit to Makomako we travelled back together on the shearer's truck. In the middle sat Tuini singing. Twenty voices joined in with gusto. Someone offered her a guitar but she turned it down. She just continued singing. With the next song she had changed her mind, she now wanted the guitar and took it. Strumming this guitar, she was completely part of her people; as they were singing her songs she could see how they experienced them, what feelings were stirred. After thousands of years of civilisation European poets are still dreaming of rediscovering this lost unity with the people (Anon, *Te Ao Hou* No. 14, April 1956: 48).

Ngawai died on August 20 1965. At her unveiling hui in 1966 the dominant theme of the sentiments expressed was that she was a genius, unique, and that her like would never be seen again. Her great contribution as a composer of around 300 songs would live on:

> many of which had become classics, and the stories behind them were retold and relived during the hui. Her compositions comprise action songs and songs of lament, love, war and comedy. (Anon, *Te Ao Hou* No. 55 June, 1966: 38)

In *The Oxford History of New Zealand Literature in English* Jane McRae, writing on Ngawai, says that:

> an account of her life and texts of many of her waiata are to be found in Ngoi Pewhairangi's *Tuini. Her Life and Her Songs* (Te Rau Press, Gisborne, 1985), a book compiled and published by her tribe who wished to preserve her work for future generations (McRae, 1998: 19).

Apart from Patricia Grace and J.C. Sturm, both of whom contributed to *Te Ao Hou* during the 1960s, there was not much evidence to suggest that Māori women made any impact on the New Zealand mainstream 'literary' scene during the period of this study.

However, Grace had work published in the 1960s in the *School Journal* and along with Ihimaera signalled a shift in the way Māori were to be seen in the literary world. It may seem odd that Sturm was not among the regular writers for the *School Journal*, as her husband, Baxter, was on the editorial staff. But as she said in the film 'Broken Journey' in the 1950s and 1960s she felt she was 'not a poet' as she thought she was not in the same league as her famous husband and his literary friends. As Gregory O'Brien notes in *A Nest of Singing Birds*:

> While the 1948 series *Life in the Pā* and the 1960 Māori Issue of the *Journal* had been largely produced by Pākehā,[29] the significant shift during the 1960s and early 70s was the upsurge in Māori contributors. During that period, Witi Ihimaera and Patricia Grace became prominent names in the *School Journal*, their writing deliberately setting out to fill the void they had personally felt as young Māori reading the *Journal*. Both contributed first-hand accounts of Māori experience in the contemporary world (O'Brien, 2007: 71).

Renée

I am a personal friend of Renée Taylor, playwright and novelist of Māori descent. For the purposes of this study I asked her to write something about her career. She responded by e-mail and I quote from her reflections in this section. Renée Taylor became a dramatist of repute in the 1980s and has since used the name Renée as both her pen name and the name she prefers to be known as generally, with no surname attached. While most people in the New Zealand literary world know Renée as a feminist dramatist and fiction writer who began writing plays in 1979, at the age of 50,[30] her literary life began much earlier.

Renée was born in Napier in 1929 and is of Ngāti Kahungunu and Irish-English-Scots ancestry. Renée left school and started work at an early age and has worked in woollen mills, a printing factory, a grocery-dairy, and as a feature writer and reviewer. Renée has described herself as a 'lesbian feminist with socialist working-class ideals' and most of her writing is a direct expression of that conviction. Much of her writing is also an expression of her Māori background, especially as the initial inspiration for her becoming a writer came through reading such publications as *Te Ao Hou*. In the late 1950s Renée was living in Greenmeadows (just out of Napier), Hawke's Bay, in her 20s, married, with three sons. Her then husband was a hard worker and a good father to the kids. She continues:

> When I decided to begin writing I knew clearly that I wanted to write to sell. I wanted to be a writer whose work editors paid for. So I started to write, at first light, funny, domestically based articles. I read every article of that kind I could get and began. My husband bought me a second-hand typewriter and I was away. I got rejections at first but quite soon acceptances. These were from the *New Zealand Free Lance*, the *Hawkes Bay Herald-Tribune*. I read about a group called the Hawkes Bay Branch of the New Zealand Women Writers' Society and I rang up the secretary of the local branch at the time, Eve Ebbett,

---

[29] Margaret Orbell contributed many retellings of Māori legends to the *School Journal* during the 1960s. She was also editor of *Te Ao Hou* from 1961 to 1965, and in 1978 she edited a book *Māori Poetry: An Introductory Anthology*. Another Pākehā writer, Barry Mitcalfe, had preceded Orbell by producing a book of translations, *Poetry of the Māori*, in 1961.

[30] Until recently few plays by New Zealand playwrights have been published in book form. In the 1970s there were editions of James K. Baxter's plays commissioned by the Globe Theatre in Dunedin. One book titled *Five New Zealand Plays* was published in 1962. Interesting, of the four playwrights represented, three are women.

who wrote light romances (under the name Eva Burfield) that were published in England, and who also later wrote other non-fiction works, among them *When the Boys Were Away.* Rachel McAlpine interviewed her for *The Passionate Pen* (Renée to Michael O'Leary, 1/2/2010).

Eve Ebbett invited Renée over to Hastings and asked her to bring her work. By then Renée had a fairly substantial pile of published and unpublished stories and articles. Ebbett always remembered and told the story many times of Renée arriving at her place and when she opened the door, she saw this young woman with this huge pile of paper under her arm, and Ebbett said of Renée 'I knew then she would make it'.

Renée submitted her application, along with three published articles, and was accepted as an associate member of the New Zealand Women Writers' Society. She joined the Hawkes Bay Branch, and in between meetings wrote as much as she could. She sold stories to the *Mirror*, a glossy magazine of the time, continued selling articles to newspapers and later to a magazine called *Eve*. Renée says:

> I read *Te Ao Hou* and anything else I could find which published works by Māori. When we moved to Wairoa, I began to research and investigate the Māori side of my family – and also wrote a weekly article for the *Wairoa Star*. While I was in Wairoa, I decided to study towards a BA degree (Renée to Michael O'Leary, 1/2/2010).

Renée had left school at twelve to go to work, and wanted to give herself this present of higher education. It took her ten years, because she could only take 2 papers a year. She did her last papers at Auckland University, and after graduation decided it was time to do the one job in theatre she had never done. Renée wrote:

> I had been working in theatre since I was in my early 30s and had done every job one could possibly do from front of house, designing sets, painting sets, acting, directing, prompting, making cups of tea, you name it, I'd done it (Renée to Michael O'Leary, 1/2/2010).

Subsequently she has been involved with community theatre, the Broadsheet Collective, PEN, radio shows, programme organisation for the Globe Theatre in Dunedin, and with script writing for TV.

In this chapter I have considered the constraints on the work of selected Māori women writers, all of whom, had they been able to publish in mainstream literary anthologies and journals in the period 1945-70 mayhave significantly changed the direction of indigenous New Zealand writing. It appears from both Sturm's own words and Ihimaera's later appraisal of her place in New Zealand literature that the work and thought of Aotearoa/New Zealand Māori women writers were both active and alive during the 1950s and 1960s but were also limited by their lack of publication opportunities and family and personal commitments.

Even Arapera Blank winning a prize in the Katherine Mansfield Memorial Competition did not translate into mainstream acceptance. Were it not for *Te Ao Hou* many Māori writers, including Sturm and Blank, conceivably would not have entered into 'the world of light' at all. That Renée not only identifies as a Māori writer but is also one of our foremost lesbian writers leads into the next chapter on lesbian writing.

Chapter 9

Lesbian Writing in New Zealand

In this section I consider lesbian writing and the representation of lesbian characters and subject matter in New Zealand literature 1945-1970. This broad approach reflects the reality of pre-1970 lesbian life in New Zealand. Many women did not overtly state their sexual identity although their work, in retrospect, does reveal a lesbian perspective for some readers. The 'closeted' nature of lesbian and gay lives in the pre-1970 era has been examined by Wellington academic, Alison Laurie). She writes: 'Though the term 'lesbian' remains the oldest term still in use for women's same-sexual relationships, the meaning changed following the influence of lesbian feminism'. Laurie states:

> I use the term 'lesbian' as Terry Castle suggests, in the dictionary sense of a woman 'whose primary emotional and erotic allegiance' is to other women [Castle 1993, p.15], and my use is not intended to suggest post-1970 political meanings or forms of self-identification for the women in this study. Rich [1980] used the idea of a 'lesbian continuum' to include 'woman-identified experience' whether sexual or not (Laurie, 2003: 24).

Laurie says definitions of lesbianism that do not take account of the strategies of invisibility, silence, deception and discretion necessary for pre-1970 lesbian survival, prevent scholars from locating earlier lesbian lives, and this is certainly the case of some of the New Zealand women writers of the period 1945-1970.

While there is evidence to suggest over the years that many women's 'primary emotional' life may be directed to their women friends, this may not be their primary 'erotic allegiance'. Examples of these close relationships can be found in memoirs such as Burgess' personal portrait of Eileen Duggan. An example from another era can be found in Ellen A. Proctor's beautifully written memoir of the English pre-Raphaelite poet Christina G. Rossetti. These examples reflect Rich's earlier comment that such intimate personal relationships are 'woman-identified experience' whether sexual or not, as Laurie observed.

Laurie quotes Emily Hamer who argues that 'one is a lesbian if the life that one lives is a lesbian life' suggesting identifying the life as lesbian, rather than the woman. She recommends that scholars should decide women were lesbian, when that is 'the best explanation of their lives', pointing out that, 'the standard of visibility is not a universal prerequisite for knowledge'. Laurie continues by quoting Lillian Faderman:

> Many women's lives were engaged in a necessary performance of heterosexuality by 'donning women's drag (both literally and figuratively)', in order to allay social suspicions (Faderman, 1999 p10) ... they lived lives of invisibility and silence to protect their lovers and their relationships (Laurie, 2003: 25).

The visibility of lesbians in early New Zealand literature was not necessarily through the publication of lesbian women's writing, but through lesbian characters that emerged in fiction by men and heterosexual or bisexual women writers. As Lawrence Jones notes:

> Lesbian characters have likewise been brought into the open in the 1980s and 1990s, no longer treated indirectly as in Sargeson's 'I for One ...'. Lesbian relationships occur at least as a secondary theme in such novels as [Marilyn] Duckworth's *A Message from Harpo* and *Seeing Red*, [Barbara] Anderson's

Girl's High, Stephanie Johnson's *The Heart's Wild Surf*, Michael O'Leary's *Straight* (1985), and Noel Virtue's *Always the Islands of Memory*. Most of these depictions are sympathetic or, more tellingly, neutral in the sense that lesbianism is simply one of the aspects of a character to be noted (Jones, 1998: 201).

I focus on women whose writing and subject matter helped create a pathway for future lesbian writing. These women writers, although most not within the period of this thesis, became the voice for 'the other' in female characters in New Zealand fiction: they are, in the following order: Ursula Bethell, Eve Langley, Jane Mander, Katherine Mansfield, Ngaio Marsh, Esma North and Marjory Nicholls. Each wrote strong female characters who aspired to become artists, writers and/or women of independent means, reflecting a growing dissatisfaction among some women of a life as a mere handmaiden or wife to a man. None were overt about their attraction to women as lovers, although many of them had sentiments and characters in their work that inferred love between women.

Aorewa McLeod, in a paper published in *Lesbian Studies in Aotearoa* uses Castle's concept of 'ghosting' lesbians to inform her study of New Zealand's 'lost lesbian writers and artists', giving as examples the lives of Margaret Escott, Jane Mander and Ngaio Marsh. She discusses New Zealand novelists, a poet, and a painter, whose identities as lesbians have been obliterated in biographies and critical commentaries. She considers whether the small and largely mono-cultural New Zealand literary and artistic scene made both coming out and being identified as a lesbian more difficult than in Europe or the United States. McLeod concludes that even in the 1990s, 'ghosting' lesbians of the past was still prevalent.

Castle suggests a ghost is something absent, immaterial, not palpable. If one thinks of a ghost as something that keeps appearing, keeps exerting an influence, something that has the power to haunt us, this is what McLeod implies as the position of women writing about lesbian experience in New Zealand literature. McLeod reminds us that 'Mander, Marsh, Escott, and in the art world Hodgkins, all lived before second wave feminism and gay liberation came to New Zealand in the early 1970s and made lesbian visibility possible'. In the 'Other' category McLeod argues that New Zealand writers were silenced by being 'ghosted', in the sense that Castle observes, not specifically acknowledged or examined as lesbian writing, including Mander, Escott, and Bethell. Some were ridiculed as being 'unwomanly', for example, by Fairburn.

Laurie states that though lesbian sexual acts were not criminalized in New Zealand, lesbianism was 'contained, regulated and controlled through a variety of mechanisms, including the fear of forced medical treatment, social exclusion and disgrace, as well as the loss of employment, housing and family relationships'. While we have seen elsewhere in this thesis that these fears were not confined to lesbian women, but in some times the confines heterosexual women had placed on them, lesbians were even more affected. Class and race were also significant determinants.

Laurie writes of the secrecy and silence of self-censorship that often meant the deliberate destruction of written records such as letters or diaries, by women themselves, or later by family members and friends to hide the perceived shame of a lesbian relationship; again this is not unique to lesbianism. For example, in her short story 'The Day of the Funeral', Isobel Andrews' character Della, who has been at the beck and call of an old aunt for several years whose funeral is the subject of the title, in an internal monologue says: 'As soon as this business is over I'm going to clean out that room. I'm going to burn all those letters. I'm going to send all that lace to a junk shop'.

Laurie concludes that the private lesbianism of most pre-1970 lesbian lives cannot be understood in isolation, and that scholars must move beyond the women's masquerades to place their lives into a lesbian context in order to recognize and understand them. She argues:

> Each life informs an understanding of the others and by considering them together the study provides a picture of lesbianism in pre-1970 New Zealand, with the stories of the narrators illuminating the written experiences. Silences should not be mistaken for absences, or heterosexuality assumed for all pre-1970 New Zealand women (Laurie, 2003: 4).

It is with these thoughts in mind that I approach the writers and their work by linking their biographical evidence to their writing to show the interconnections between real life experiences of the writers and experiences expressed through creative fiction. Pre-1970s offerings in fiction on any kind of homosexuality were subdued and meagre.[31] Mansfield's stories contain some lesbian themes. However, until women like Ngahuia Te Awakotuku, Miriam Saphira and Cathie Dunsford in the 1970s and 1980s announced themselves as lesbians, it was difficult to know whether women writers identified as lesbians or not.

Another woman in the struggle to have women's work taken seriously is poet Heather McPherson of the Spiral Collective. McPherson is a personal friend and I have published her work. Early in her career she realised that she would have to take up the fight against the male establishment when she told Leo Bensemann, then editor of *Landfall*, that she had a collection of poetry and would he look at them; his response has been recorded earlier in the abstract to this thesis and it was in the face of negative attitudes like his towards feminism (even though Bensemann said her poems were publishable) that she knew the battle lines were drawn.

McPherson states that after joining a group to fight for homosexual law reform 'with a number of talented women artists in the group, with their stories being turned down for publication or by art galleries, I thought I would rather be working with/for women artists'. Thus the Spiral Collective was formed to provide an alternative to the male literary and artistic establishment.

What follows is a brief study of some of the writers around the time of this study who have been claimed in recent years by women's groups and academics as being part of the lesbian canon in the literary history of New Zealand. As noted earlier one interesting aspect this thesis has looked at is that while the period 1945 to 1970 provides virtually no overtly or even covertly lesbian literature, there is evidence that pre-1945 women writers were recognised as having intimate relationships with other women, whether sexual or not remains in the realm of speculation.

Ursula Bethell
While not strictly from the period this study covers, Bethell died at Christchurch in 1945, she is an example of the often ambiguous nature of some women's lives, and her oft presumed 'lesbian' lifestyle had an influence on later generations of writers. Having lived in England during WW1 Bethell returned home to Christchurch and built a house in Cashmere, 'Rose Cottage', where she lived for 10 years with Effie Pollen, a younger woman who came from Wellington to be with her. At the age of 50 Bethell began writing poetry. While Bethell mentored poets and artists of the time,

---

[31] James Courage's *The Fifth Child* (1948) and *A Way of Love* (1959) have homosexual themes, as do several of Frank Sargeson's pre-1970s stories – 'The hole that Jack dug', 'I for one', 'I saw in my dream', 'I've lost my pal' and 'That summer'.

Pollen kept the house in what was an almost 'traditional' marriage situation, although visitors commented that each woman had her own room.

After Pollen died suddenly in 1934[32] Bethell was devastated, writing a 'Memorial' poem to her every year for the next six years on or around the anniversary. These poems of grief to her have become an intimate and lasting gesture of love to the woman she shared her life with. There is no formal acknowledgement of any specific 'lesbian' relationship between the two women and perhaps her Christian beliefs meant that she could possibly never acknowledge this even to herself.

The question may be asked: Was Bethell's sexuality a deterrent to publication? It is difficult to say - because in one sense, it was her class that allowed her to live in a lifestyle that encouraged her creative work as well as a partner who supported her in her creative lifestyle - making meals, hosting friends and family while Bethell was the hostess, the centre of attention. Bethell is recognised as one of the pioneers of modern New Zealand poetry. Like others of her generation she was forced to confront the tension between her English origins and sympathies and her New Zealand milieu. In addition she was drawn to examine the disjunctions between religious certainty and everyday experience. Her attempts at developing a poetic voice to express her enlarged understanding were bold and innovative; in all her observations she looked with new eyes.

In a letter to Holcroft, Bethell described the relationship with Pollen as 'prevailingly maternal' – a bond of mutual protection and support. She also expressed similar views to fellow poet John Summers and theatre director Rodney Kennedy. Whiteford contends that it has become increasingly common in recent years to interpret the relationship between the two women as lesbian; Bethell's description of it as 'prevailingly maternal' is read, if not as a deliberate subterfuge, then as a way of explaining physical tenderness between women.

Whatever the nature of their relationship, Pollen's death further affected Bethell in that it made it almost impossible for her to write any further poetry. Whiteford states that Bethell confessed in a letter to Eileen Duggan:

> *Time and Place* ... is made up of things written about the same time as the Garden pieces – in the same burst of excitement – of joy. ... Now I am a tree struck by lightning – dead. I can think things, but not feel them. One must feel to write. All joy is lost ... As I wander about these mountain roads I try to pray, and to know that prayers are heard when they seem not to be. It is all pain ... & a sense of failure – I am told that purgatory begins in this world ... You know I think one has to write – about anything – out of faith – great poets may write out of great grief – but faith must impel the little ones. If I could find that again – or even a lively hope instead of a faint one! (Bethell in Whiteford, 2008: no pagination).

There is, of course, no way of knowing for certain what was the nature of the relationship between the two women, and the question is complicated by the debate over whether the term 'lesbian' should be applied only to sexual relationships or more generally to social, celibate relationships. Her personal life may always be a mystery but there is no question that her primary emotional and intimate life was with another woman. She came through that pain and grief to once again create new work and to be acknowledged by her peers as a strong force in New Zealand's literary history. However, for many years, and for some modern critics, Bethell's work has not been regarded as lesbian writing.

---

[32] It is interesting to note that Effie Pollen is buried about 200 yards from the poet Marjory Nicholls in Wellington's Karori Cemetery.

Eve Langley

One very interesting example of a woman writer whose career covers the whole time period of this thesis and who chose to live an unconventional literary life was Eve Langley. Australian by birth she came to live in Northcote, New Zealand, where she became friends with Gloria Rawlinson, Hyde and Sargeson. The alternative life she lived as a man does not necessarily mean that Langley was lesbian, but she was certainly an alternative thinker. She was known to have affairs with women and wrote about it in her poetry and fiction. Langley worked as a journalist, a travelling bookseller, and then a gardener and housemaid at a hostel in Whanganui. Around 1934 she moved to Carterton, where she met Luigi Rinaldi, a car salesman. In 1935 at Auckland she had his child (who died shortly after birth). Afterwards she met an art student, Hilary Roy Clark, whom she married in 1937. Although 32, she gave her age as 28; he was 22. The couple were to have three children.

During the 1930s Langley had begun writing poetry and short stories, and these were widely published in New Zealand periodicals. In 1938 Hyde wrote, 'Eve Langley … has colour and a swift imagery, which changes shape in her exotic mind without effort or strain'. In 1940, while living in extreme poverty with two small children on Auckland's North Shore she wrote her first novel, *The Pea Pickers*. It is based on her and her sister June's experiences as cross-dressing itinerant farm labourers (Steve and Blue) in Gippsland in the late 1920s.

In 1954 Angus and Robertson, the Australian publishers of *The Pea Pickers*, published its sequel, *White Topee*. In a short episode Eve/Steve tells an Italian cobber that she is really Oscar Wilde reborn as a woman. That year Langley claimed that she had changed her name by deed poll to Oscar Wilde. Angus and Robertson refused to publish her next novel, *Wild Australia*, where a Wilde narrative takes over the last third of the novel. This intriguing obsession dominates Joy L. Thwaite's 1989 biography of Langely.

After the rejection of *Wild Australia*, Langley set two more novels in Australia and based her others on the journals she had kept since her arrival in New Zealand. They are, like *The Pea Pickers*, first-person narratives beginning with Eve/Steve's arrival in New Zealand and ending in 1941 when she has two children and is pregnant again. The readers for Angus and Robertson rejected the 10 novels written by Langley in the 1950s and 1960s as 'purely personal' and as showing a 'most insensitive lack of reticence in her private affairs'. Thus, these Australian publishers are shown to have the same reluctance to use the 'personal experience' as a valid literary device, and as discussed in the chapter on women poets, ignore the 'female' impetus in literature.

McLeod states, however, that this is what gives the novels a powerful and fascinating insight into a disastrous marriage and the conflict Langley experienced between her responsibilities as a wife and mother and her attempted career as a writer. A friend of Robin Hyde and Gloria Rawlinson, and an observer of the Elam art scene, she provides glimpses in her unpublished novels of the bohemian literary and artistic fringes of Auckland, as well as vivid portrayals of places and buildings, such as Partington's Mill, where as a student her lover, Hilary, had a room. The unpublished typescripts of Langely's novels are held in the Mitchell Library, Sydney.

Langley died alone, sometime between 1-13 June 1974, in a cottage at North Katoomba in the Blue Mountains, where her body was found about a month later. Ruth Park in her 1992 autobiography, *A Fence around the Cuckoo* writes of meeting Langley in 1940:

> a dazzling autodidact with a head full of classical literature, other languages, and uncontrollable creativity the frustration of which was eventually to drive

her mad; ... to me she was a living example of all that was rapturous, exciting, literary (Park in McLeod, 2007: no pagination).

Again, Langley's work is seldom read as 'lesbian writing' nor is this lens used to interpret her writing.

Jane Mander

Novelist Jane Mander died in 1949. She is known primarily for her novel, *The Story of a New Zealand River*. The furore over the themes of love and sexuality that this book focused on shocked the parochial small town sensibilities of the New Zealand literary scene and her work was not well treated at the time. This novel was set in the lush bush clad surroundings of this area and evokes the author's love of nature. Her father was one of the early entrepreneurs in North Auckland and after running the mill he tried his hand at politics and the press, buying the *Northern Advocate* newspaper, which gave his daughter a chance to write – she worked as a reporter and sub-editor and eventually ran the editorial office herself.

Mander spent time in Sydney as a freelance journalist but had aspirations to study at Columbia University and at the age of 35 she sailed for New York, travelling via London, carrying with her the script of a novel which she offered to four publishers, all of whom declined it. At Columbia University, she achieved the highest grades in examinations at the end of her first and second years, a remarkable feat given that she also held numerous part-time jobs including lecturing, coaching younger students, and writing for magazines to supplement her income.

During this time she continued to rework her novel but after another rejection, finally abandoned it. Financial pressure and overwork exacerbated her poor health, and she was forced to abandon her studies in her third year. Known for her liberal feminism, she joined the suffrage movement in 1915 and campaigned for the New York State referendum on women's franchise. During this time she worked on a new novel, which was accepted by John Lane in 1917 and published in 1920: *The Story of a New Zealand River*.

While well received in England and the USA, *The Story of a New Zealand River* was poorly reviewed in New Zealand. Lacking precedents for a local literature, critics reproved the novel's failure to conform to the familiar conventions of the nineteenth century regional British novel in theme and content. Reviewers expected documentary literalism in a novel so liberally sprinkled with real place names and details of actual events. Many readers found the novel too outspoken on matters of sex and religion. The *New Zealand Herald*, in 1920, proclaimed The River's liberal ending 'too early for good public morality'; it was set aside in the 'Reserve' section of libraries to be borrowed by approved adults only on special request to the librarian.

Mander's next three novels were all set in New Zealand, drawing directly on her childhood experiences of pioneering life in the north. *The Passionate Puritan* (1921) is a rather cheerful account of kauri milling, apparently written with an eye on the cinema, 'a mistake', Mander claimed, she 'ever afterwards regretted'. Critical attention focused on Mander's purported failure to portray convincingly 'representative' members of the communities she chose to sketch, on her putative moral deviance, and her continued obsession with what was labelled 'the sex problem'. Mander responded from London to her critics in a letter to the *Auckland Star* in 1924:

> a writer who is trying to be an artist, as I sincerely am, has nothing whatsoever to do with being a tourist agent, or a photographer, or a historian, or a compiler of community statistics. I am simply trying to be honest and loyal to my own experience ... as a matter of fact I'm not half sexy enough for

thousands of readers here (Mander in McGregor, DNZB, 2007: no pagination).

Having championed the advances of New Zealand abroad for two decades, Mander was now bitterly disappointed in her country, which to her mind had failed to fulfil its potential and had become 'one of the backward people of the earth'. The puritanical malaise, so often attacked in her New Zealand novels, was a condition she now found rampant, threatening to dissipate the energies and promise of the pioneers. It is deeply ironical that it is precisely this puritanical, imitative colonialism, which marked the response of her original New Zealand readers to her novels. Illness, years of pedestrian literary work, and an intolerant local audience combined to whither her creativity.

Some women novelists of this time like Mander treated sexual themes far more openly and daringly than their contemporary male counterparts and often argued for 'free love'. For example, Jean Devanny's *The Butcher's Shop* in 1926 described a loveless marriage, and her heroine's extramarital relationship as 'clean', because it was motivated by love and her book was banned as a result. Hyde in *The Godwits Fly* in 1938 juxtaposed 'the glory hole', or sex, with 'the glorybox', or marriage: neither was satisfactory for women, but love may be worth it. McLeod discusses lesbian readings of Mander's 1920 novel *The Story of a New Zealand River* and Escott's 1936 novel *Showdown*. *The New Zealand Women's Weekly* and other magazines included romance stories reinforcing the ideals of Hollywood and the belief that women should marry for love having met 'Mr Right'. These representations reinforced ideas of the 'companionate marriage', added to by love-songs played on the radio.

And McLeod suggests that there were New Zealand connections during this period of lesbian awareness in New York. For example, McLeod says that Jane Mander lived in Greenwich Village from:

> 1912 near Willa Cather, affirming, 'we had something of a little set of our own in Greenwich Village'. She moved on to London in 1920, describing 'getting to know Radclyffe Hall and the Sackville Wests' before returning to New Zealand in 1934 (McLeod, 2001: 51).

Mander writes with an intimate sense of belonging to this country and a fervent love of it; her work is undistorted by either exaggerated enthusiasm or the colonial cultural cringe. From financial necessity she wrote articles, reviewed books for the *Mirror* and the *Monocle* and gave radio talks on a variety of topics.

Mander associated with literary figures not only overseas. In New Zealand she also knew other writers such as Holcroft, Sargeson, Roderick Finlayson, D'Arcy Cresswell and Hyde, and even experienced writers valued her critical appraisal of their work. In a landmark series of articles which appeared in the Christchurch *Press* in 1934 she advised New Zealand novelists on how to break away from the local pitfalls of too much scenery and sentiment. Her humour, her vigour, and her respect for worthwhile writing is evident in these essays and in all her journalism. She was a founding member of the PEN New Zealand Centre and honorary vice president of the New Zealand Women Writers' and Artists' Society from 1932 until her death in 1949.

> Although her output is relatively small, her reputation as a novelist has grown since her death. Other contemporary writers addressed social issues in a local context, but few matched Jane Mander's technical facility, candour, and insight into personal relationships (McGregor in DNZB, 2007: website).

Katherine Mansfield

Another woman writer to explore lesbian experiences was this country's most celebrated writer. Although she is outside my timeframe Mansfield was one of the first 'voices' of New Zealand women to represent a lifestyle that was independent, professional and creative and had a major effect on inspiring other New Zealand women to write what they thought and felt. She was friends with The Bloomsbury Group in London who admired the elegance of her short story writing. Yet the themes of her work took her back to her childhood and the New Zealand landscape.

During her short life she was part of the literary circles of the time including Virginia Woolf, DH Lawrence & Frieda, who became her closest friends, and aspects of Mansfield's personality have inspired fictional characters in D. H. Lawrence's *Women in love*, Aldous Huxley's *Point counter point*, Francis Carco's *Les innocents* and Conrad Aiken's 'Your obituary well written'. Her long-term relationship with John Middleton-Murray led to many collaborations between the two as writers, critics and editors. However, Mansfield explored lesbian relationships in her work and had strong relationships with women throughout her life.

For example, she had a close relationship with a Māori girl who she met at school and some of her stories reflect the intimacy and eroticism of their early encounters with their burgeoning sexuality. This relationship was with Maata Mahupuku, a Māori woman Mansfield met in Wellington, and then again in London. In Mansfield's story 'Bliss' she indicates the first consciousness of unspoken feelings between women. This 'knowing' of women's intimacy was rarely written about and Mansfield was one of the first New Zealand writers to articulate a deep insight into other women's emotional and psychosexual attraction.

Mansfield wrote of passion, relationships, abandonment and emotional turmoil that resonated with a new generation of readers in New Zealand wanting to find something tangible in a culture rooted in parochialism and dominated by sport. Mansfield's literary prowess was something to hold onto. In spite of her own conviction that she would not be 'fashionable' for long Mansfield has acquired an international reputation as a writer of short stories, poetry, letters, journals and reviews, but is not mostly read as 'lesbian writing', and even stories like 'Bliss' are not generally interpreted as such.

Ngaio Marsh

Edith Ngaio Marsh was born in Christchurch on April 23, 1895, only 45 years after the Canterbury province was founded. While still a child, the family moved to the house in Cashmere, about 700m from the home of Ursula Bethell, where she lived for the rest of her life. Her talents lay in three directions; painting, the theatre, and crime fiction. Marsh remains an enigmatic figure in the annals of New Zealand women writers. On one level she is still, perhaps, the New Zealand writer best known outside this country as discussed earlier.

Yet, despite her success she appears to have felt she failed to get on terms with herself. It has been suggested that it was her sexuality that was responsible for her unease. Wevers, in a review of Joanne Drayton's (2008) biography of Marsh, writes:

> The mystery of Ngaio Marsh remains unsolved. When Ngaio Marsh's autobiography *Black Beech and Honeydew,* first published in 1965[6], was considered for a reprint in 1980, Collins' Crime Club editor Elizabeth Walter panned the idea. She thought the original book 'pretty dull' and noted that if you are going to write an autobiography you have to be prepared to 'let your hair down a little'. Joanne Drayton's *Ngaio Marsh: Her Life in Crime* seems to

promise that it will let something down, billing itself as 'the ultimate detective story – revealed for the first time', and featuring a chic and androgynous Marsh on its cover. But what really does it reveal? (Wevers, 2008: Nov 15-21).

Wevers points out that Drayton's big revelation is that Marsh's most significant emotional relationships were with women and may also have been sexual, is impossible to verify or make personal. Wevers concludes that while Marsh was a larger-than-life figure, whose legacy to New Zealand was considerable, it will be a 'Died in the Wool' fan who wants to absorb so much detail about her, and at the end, what will they really know that they didn't know (or guess) before?

Drayton's is not the first biography of Marsh. Margaret Lewis (1991) *Ngaio Marsh: A Life*, does not reveal Marsh's private life. Marsh herself comments in her autobiography that 'I have deflected my own reticence' (Marsh, 1966: 284) and she took pains to destroy evidence – every letter from her friend Doris McIntosh, for instance. However, there is evidence that she certainly found expressions of the 'other' interesting, even if she was not a participant. For example, on her first visit to England in 1928, which lasted five years, she frequented London clubs and was fascinated to see:

> almost always alone, at a table just inside the door, sat a strange figure: an old, old man with a flower in his coat who looked as if he had been dehydrated like a specimen leaf and then rouged a little. No one ever accompanied him or paused at his table. He looked straight before him and at intervals raised his glass in a frog's hand and touched his lips with it.
> One night we asked the restaurateur who he was.
> 'A poet,' said Signor Vecchi, 'and once, long ago I understand, a celebrated personage. It is Lord Alfred Douglas' (Marsh, 1966: 201).

He was the lover of Oscar Wilde. On a trip to Monte Carlo, Marsh saw for the first time transvestites and transsexuals and women dressed as men on stage. She observed:

> Ladies ... of a kind that was entirely new to me. The croupiers referred to the most dominant of them as 'cette monsieur-dame'. She seemed to be having quite a pleasant time of it, running her finger round inside her collar and settling her tie. She wore a sort of habit and was perhaps by Isherwood out of Huxley. The disconcerting thing about many of the habitués was their tendency to seem as if they had been written by somebody not quite on the top of his form (Marsh, 1966: 208).

Her 33 novels with her main character policeman Roderick Alleyn, who was described in a sketch she included in one manuscript, handsome but surprisingly feminine. This writing could be regarded as 'lesbian' with Alleyn as an alter-ego for herself.

In 1977 the Mystery Writers of America gave her their highest honour, naming her a Grand Master (she joked about not being a Grand Mistress). Marsh was created a Dame in 1966. And while her autobiography gives nothing away and she publicly denied being a lesbian, doubts remain. New Zealand novelist Stevan Eldred-Grigg suggests the very fact that she 'over-invented herself' is indicative. His 1997 novel *Blue Blood* explores the idea that she was lesbian. She was widely supposed to be lesbian on the stereotypical basis of her deep voice and her habit of wearing trousers, and lifelong friend, Sylvia Fox, lived in a bungalow just above her house. Analysing her work as 'lesbian writing' could bring new perspectives to Marsh's work, but is outside the scope of this study.

Esma North and Marjory Lydia Nicholls

Both Esma North, born in 1892, and Marjory Nicholls, born in 1891, attended Wellington Girls' College, where Nicholls edited the school magazine, and was regarded as one of the best known and best loved girls of the school. Both women became teachers and in North's case she became principal of Wellington Girls College. At Victoria University College Nicholls was the first woman to win the Plunkett Medal for oratory, produced two Drama Society plays and was active in various other groups, though did not complete a degree.

Nicholls went overseas and in England studied stage production with Edith (Edy) Craig who lived in a lesbian *ménage a trois* with Christopher St John and Claire (Tony) Atwood. Edith founded the Barn Theatre at Smallhythe which attracted a lesbian circle, including Radclyffe Hall, Una Troubridge, Vita Sackville-West, Winaretta (Singer) de Polignac, Ethel Smyth and other lesbian suffragists which connects Nicholls to a prominent British lesbian network.

Back in New Zealand Nicholls studied painting with Dorothy Kate Richmond. She lived in her own flat in Sydney Street, Wellington, and was a close friend of poet Eileen Duggan who, despite being deeply religious, may also have had lesbian relationships. Nicholls published three volumes of poetry: *A Venture in Verse* (1917), *Gathered Leaves* (1922) and *Thirdly* (1929) and was well known in amateur theatre. She was run over at a bus stop in October 1930, dying at the age of 40 years. These two stanzas are from her poem 'A Would-be Wanderer':

Rest at an inn (if it come my way)
For I'll walk any road I please,
Chanting verse from Euripides,
Or Villon's ballads of yesterday.

Or loll Bohemian-wise and dream
About Verlaine or Baudelaire –
A poet strange, with pea-green hair,
Who supped, o'nights, from a skull of cream
(Nicholls, 1917: 1).

It has been suggested that this poem indicates that Nicholls was familiar with both classical and French writers on homosexuality or other forms of 'other' sexual behaviour and states her resolve to live an independent life. Living in her own flat, studying with famous lesbians, and traveling round the world, Nicholls in her short life walked the roads she pleased.

Esma North (her name was a mixture of her first and second names, Esther and Mary) published one volume of poetry, *Primroses for my Fair*, in 1930. Throughout the book there are what are nowadays called markers, hints at things that may be a sub-text to any given book or philosophy. In this case it has been suggested that much of North's work contained references to lesbian or 'other' forms of relationships between women. Indeed, Wright notes of the poem 'Human Comfort' that: 'Nowadays it would be read as a lesbian poem'.

Further indications of North's possibly lesbian interest can be found in some other poems. Two seem to be obvious echoes of Irish poet Oscar Wilde's relationship with Lord Alfred Douglas. One poem is called 'De Profundis', the title of a famous work by Wilde. Another Wildean echo can be found in North's poem, 'Hush! Beloved', in which each stanza there is a variation of the last three lines:

I'll speak, my sweet,
In whispers low. I would not have them hear

The words I breathe for my lover's ear
(North, 1930:7).

While it is true that the person North addresses is not acknowledged as a man or a woman, there is, perhaps, something of the following famous line: 'I am the Love that dare not speak its name'. Lord Alfred Douglas coined the phrase in his poem to Wilde, *Two Loves* (1896). Also the phrase 'primrose path' refers to those who are dedicated to the pursuit of pleasure, another Wildean echo. Wright throws another light on this aspect by discussing the poem, 'Lady Mine', by Marjory Nicholls. He suggests:

> For instance in the poem 'Lady Mine' the person addressed sounds real. The term Primrose-like and the account of a compassionate conservationalist read to me as a very definite reference to Esma North (Wright, 2009: 8).

Wright mentions a poem by Nicholls called 'Little Daughter' which he claims:

> Clearly tells the story of a young woman whose love affair has had a bitter outcome. By 1911 Marjory Nicholls was 20 years old ... don't rule anything out (Wright, 2009: 13).

So whether Nicholls and North were lesbian lovers as young women in either a strict or open definition of the term cannot be ruled out. While there is no definitive biographical evidence the speculation is valid given the circumstantial and literary evidence.

That both Nicholls and North were seen as being of the much vilified 'Georgian School' by the writers and publishers whose views took precedence in the late 1930s has meant that their obscurity in the New Zealand literary canon since that time was assured; that they were also women added to their being marginalised. The main reason that the majority of the women I have written on lesbian writers fall outside my time frame, 1945 to 1970, is because that it was only women writing on either side of the years mentioned who wrote with any openness about their lives in the sexual sense. This is quite understandable when we observe some of the male attitudes prevalent at the time, manifested by Fairburn who wrote feminists:

> have so bedevilled the man-woman situation that only the most arrant sentimentalist is likely to be applauded. Any writer who tries to import a little common sense into that situation is asking to be lynched by the moustached Amazons of the women's journals and the millions who abide by their word. (Fairburn, 1967: 22-23)

Like many women writers of the period 1945-1970 women writing about lesbian matters hid their thoughts and feelings. The fact that women were writers at all was often seen in a disparaging and condescending way by both male writers and publishers. Add to that the 'perversion' of deviant sexual practices and they must have feared a double rejection slip in the mail. No writers felt comfortable with this subject matter until after this period, and for those who did write on such topics the lesbianism was either ignored, as in Mansfield's 'Bliss', or the work was not regarded as significant, as in North's poems.

Thus, while there is not much evidence of lesbian writing available during the period of this study there is a likelihood that women writers who were 'lesbian' did not want to openly express their sexual and emotional preference for fear of being ridiculed and ostracised by those in the literary scene and in society as a whole. The next chapter is about a genre that many in the literary world have considered a woman's domain, that of writing for children. I argue that the politics of who and what got published in this field often mirrors the male dominated area of the other literary traditions covered thus far in this thesis, for example the *School Journal*.

Chapter 10

Children's Writers
This chapter considers the women writers who wrote children's stories. I look at the career of Elsie Locke, and discuss how the *School Journal* and the Publications sector of the Department of Education gave a significant forum for many of the writers who later went on to be among our better-known writers. The chapter also looks at how the *School Journal*, for example, encouraged writers like Frame when she was a child in Oamaru to want to become a writer herself. It allowed her and others like her, to believe that such a thing was possible, even in New Zealand.

Anyone studying *The Oxford Companion to New Zealand Literature* for children's literature between 1945 and 1970 by either men or women writers could be forgiven for thinking that little or nothing existed in this genre during those years. There are two entries on literature for children in the book, firstly an article titled 'Children's pages' by Heather Murray that concerns itself with New Zealand newspapers which had exclusive pages set aside for children's interests. This entry names some of these papers from the 1870s through to the 1940s when 'paper shortages during World War 2 curtailed or ended many children's features and radio gave children another option for entertainment'.

The only two other children specific entries in the companion are no more than a paragraph each. The 'New Zealand Children's Literature Association' (NZCLA) was formed in 1969 to provide a 'grass-roots' approach to introduce children to books and other literature. Secondly, there is the 'New Zealand Children's Book Foundation' (Te Maataa Pukapuka Tamariki o Aotearoa) that was established in 1990 as a part of the New Zealand Book Council to promote children's books, and encourage reading by children. Of course, this does not tell the whole story and many of the women writers who appear in this thesis began their careers writing for the children's pages in daily newspapers. Murray writes: 'When books for the young were not widely available, early exposure to writing encouraged children to feel part of a lively writing community, in which Hyde, Dallas, Frame, Ruth Park, Locke and others first achieved publication' (Murray, 1998: 103). In some of the individual entries of writers in *The Oxford Companion to New Zealand Literature* the work of the writers is acknowledged in the field of writing for children.

Early reading inspires writing
And it was not just publication as adults that these book pages encouraged, but also as children some of these writers attributed the fact that newspaper children pages existed that was the reason they could entertain the notion to become writers themselves. For example, Frame in 1936, then at the age of twelve, states in volume one of her autobiography that she along with others began 'to write their own poems and stories, encouraged locally by the children's pages in the newspapers'.

In Sturm there is slightly more coverage of Children's literature, with a whole chapter dedicated to this genre. There is a sub-heading 'New Impulses, 1950-1970' which deals with the children's writing of the period of this thesis except for the years 1945 to 1950. Betty Gilderdale, who wrote the entry on children's literature, sees two main trends in books for children during this period. One is a push to establish a literature that focuses on developing New Zealand's own national identity through a literary move towards 'social realism', that is a an acknowledgement of experience of life in New Zealand as it is lived by people who live here.

Washday at the Pā

The second was the increase in books depicting Māori themes and people in a more positive, less idealized context. For example, Gilderdale states that the writers and publishers of the time aimed 'not only to show "life in New Zealand" on farm, on sea shore, and in the high country, but also to offer positive images of the Māori' (Gilderdale, 1998: 540). Jane Hill, Gay Kohlap, Pat Lawson and Valerie Salt were all involved in this sub-genre of children's writing. Ans Westra, in an interview in the September 1964 issue of 'Photography' (quoted in Gilderdale's entry), about her controversial photographic essay *Washday at the Pā*, which was withdrawn from distribution as a 1961 *School Bulletin* on the grounds that it gave the wrong impression of Māori people, her aim was to show 'what an intelligent coloured race can do with civilization when they are given a chance by being treated as human beings'.

Not withstanding the unintentional racism inherent in a phrase like 'an intelligent coloured race' Westra's approach in depicting a Māori community in a photo-journalistic manner was certainly new and challenging. Westra herself was, of course, a woman artist and writer whose work broke new ground in terms of women undertaking the kind of work she was doing since she moved to New Zealand from Europe in 1957. She was also something of a pioneer in her subject matter of showing the everyday lives of ordinary New Zealanders, and in particular using Māori and Pacific Island subjects for her photographic essays long before they became common currency.

Her early work appeared in many magazines such as *Te Ao Hou* and much of her work was for the Department of Education. It is perhaps ironic that despite her seemingly enlightened approach to Māori motifs, which often highlighted the women's roles in whānau life that the harshest criticism of her *Washday at the Pā* book came from the Māori Women's Welfare League. Gregory O'Brien in *A Nest of Singing Birds* tells of further Westra works around this time. He says she also produced 'book-length photo-essays for the [*School*] *Journal*, including *Children at Play* and *Holiday in the Capital* (both 1964) and *The Circus Comes to Town* (1965). The latter publication was an extended piece of accessible photojournalism although, as was the case with much of Westra's commissioned work, there were some remarkable pictures amidst the workaday ones'.

Elsie Locke

It could be said what Westra was doing with her camera the writer Elsie Locke was doing with her pen. Locke (1912– 2001) was a writer, novelist, historian and leader in peace movements and women's affairs, and another writer whose life covers the whole time-frame of this study. Born in Hamilton, Locke described the hardships and delights of her early life in Waiuku and at Auckland University in her autobiographical work *Student at the Gates* (1981).

> This autobiography details life in the 1920s–30s, illuminating both some dominant political and literary personalities of the time and also the influences which shaped her idealistic socialist philosophies. In the 1930s Locke edited the early feminist journal Woman Today (Hebley, 1998: 309).

Born Elsie Farelly, in 1941 she married Jack Locke, both having been members of the New Zealand Communist Party, which she left in 1956 after the Russian invasion of Hungary. They moved from Wellington to Christchurch, where they raised four children. She served on the national executive of the Campaign for Nuclear Disarmament (1957–70). She also continued writing for adults: *The Shepherd and the Scullery Maid* (1950), *The Human Conveyer Belt* (1968), *The Gaoler* (1978) on early Otago, and two privately printed family histories. She edited

Gordon Watson, New Zealander, 1912–1945 (1949). In 1959, she received the Katherine Mansfield Award for Non-Fiction for her essay in *Landfall* 48.

Locke is probably more widely known as a writer for children. Drawing her topics and themes from her interests and commitments, she carried out diligent research, often historical or relating to outdoor exercise. Her preparation included learning Te Reo Māori to understand the Māori point of view, which she expresses with sympathy and insight in novels that in this respect were in advance of general perceptions. Her first novel for children was based on a true story. *The Runaway Settlers* (1965), illustrated by Anthony Maitland, portrays a remarkable historical-fiction mother whose experiences include driving a herd of cattle over the Southern Alps and down the Teremakau River to the West Coast. This novel has been in continuous print for longer than any other New Zealand children's book.

Locke's historical novels during the period covered by this thesis include *The End of the Harbour* (1969), illustrated by Katarina Mataira, a compassionate exploration of land issues from Māori and Pākehā perspectives. Of Locke's books Gilderdale states they are 'closer, perhaps, to historical documentary than to fiction. They present Māori perspectives and are based on careful reconstructions of actual events, angled from the viewpoint of a young protagonist'.

The 1951 New Zealand Writers' Conference was part of Canterbury's Centenary celebrations, for which Locke had written *The Shepherd and the Scullery Maid.* She had also published a number of articles and poems by this time, and several of her radio talks had been broadcast. The Conference was held in Christchurch in May 1951, and Elsie was one of the few women there. Ruth France, another Canterbury woman writer, who was married to a boat-builder, also attended, but it wasn't until after the Conference that she and Locke became friends.

One day, France approached Locke in the Christchurch Public Library and told her quite frankly that she was 'starved for literary conversation'. Both had children, both had been librarians, and both were inspired to commemorate the 1951 Wellington to Lyttelton boat race, which was devastated by a violent storm. Locke wrote *For Those Who Sailed,* a series of poems, and France wrote a novel, *The Race,* published in 1958. Sometimes France wrote under the pen name Paul Henderson. France's own life suggests a degree of frustration:

> Determined to be the good wife and mother that society at the time demanded, she also spoke of the impulse towards writing, of the intensity of purpose that grew with age and excluded procrastination, and of the happiness of being alone and writing (Beaglehole, 2007: DNZB website).

Although France did not write for children the two women must have found much common ground in their lives' circumstances as they shared the double balancing act of bringing up children as well as being writers. France pre-deceased Locke by thirty-three years, dying in 1968 from cancer.

At the conference, Locke sat with Winston and Sophie Rhodes. Winston taught English at the university and often lectured for the Workers Education Association (WEA). Locke reported on the Conference in the left-wing journal *Here and Now* the following month, declaring 'The Conference confirmed that our native literature has outgrown its knobbly-kneed stage, and has the vigour of youth, if not the quality of maturity.' She expressed special gratitude for James K Baxter's address on 'Recent Trends in New Zealand Poetry' for its wisdom, its penetration, its social awareness, and its superbly phrased language.

She also mentioned addresses by Johannes C Anderson on Māori Lore; by Blackwood Paul on 'The Novel in New Zealand' and by H Winston Rhodes on William Morris and his 'art for the people and by the people.' At the end of her report, she 'unashamedly' added a footnote about the social responsibility of writers:

I am convinced that many writers find it difficult because they begin with themselves instead of with the other fellow ... The Conference revealed that, potentially at least, many of those present have much to give, even though their skill at the craft is not yet matched by their understanding of crucial human problems ... Will they succeed in cultivating and conveying the life-giving spiritual food which a young country needs at this grave yet dazzlingly hopeful point in history? (Locke, 1951: 27-28).

Locke had her first contribution to the *School Journal*, 'the Secret Rescue', published in 1958, and thereafter became a regular contributor until her death in 2001. During the intervening years she wrote many articles which reflected her commitment to social and socialist ideas. This can best be seen in her article in the Part 4 *School Journal* 1968, a year designated as the United Nations' 'Human Rights Year'. The issue had an interesting cover by artist David Cowe and was titled 'The Hopeful Peace & the Hopeful War', which echoed her 1951 article on the Writers' Convention. In the 1968 *School Journal* Locke states:

Everyone has the right to food, clothing, housing and social services ... No one shall be held in slavery or servitude ... Everyone is entitled to these rights and freedoms without distinction of sex ... Everyone has the right to freedom of thought, conscience and religion; to freedom of speech and opinion, and of peaceful assembly and association (Locke, 2007: 58).

Thus Locke enters into her children's canon the ideas and ideals of her political and social agenda. To emphasise that 'everyone is entitled to these rights and freedoms without distinction of sex' in an official 'journal' aimed at eleven and twelve year olds was quite a brave and unusual thing to do in 1968.

The School Journal
While the *School Journal* was a good outlet for New Zealand artists and writers as a place or forum to earn money by their talents, it also was a predominately male-orientated affair at least until the 1970s. For example, until 1972 when Vanya Lowry took over as editor and 'embraced the new possibilities [of technology and design] and pushed the limits', the editors were male and most of the permanent staff were also men. It is a common assumption that the majority of writers and artists in the children's literature genre are women.

However, an analysis of those who were either writing for or illustrating for the *School Journal* from its inception in 1907 and its centenary in 2007 shows that men were the most numerically represented. Thus, in its first one hundred years out of the two hundred and ninety nine artists and or writers 168 men and 131 were women, as presented in the index of the recent history of the *School Journal, A Nest of Singing Bird.'* The most famous period of literary editorship of the *School Journal* is perhaps the 1950s and 1960s when the main editor was poet Alistair Te Ariki Campbell, with the other three poets James K Baxter, Louis Johnson, and Peter Bland making a formidable foursome of the cream of New Zealand literature at the time.

While many women writers and artists, such as Ruth Dallas, Ruth Park, Evelyn Clouston and Jill McDonald, (and some like Joan Smith and Helen Shaw produced both writing and artwork) at the time were given commissioned work to do for the *Journal*, and the men above had a reputation for being sympathetic towards women writers a lot of the time, the fact remained that these men were the arbiters of taste and the ones who had the say in what and who got published.

Alongside the *School Journal* the Department of Education also commissioned and produced the school *Bulletins* which were single issue publications that allowed for social studies, geography and historical topics to be explored by children at greater length than could be done in the *Journal*. These sometimes became quite controversial, as in the *Bulletin* titled 'Te Tiriti ō Waitangi' by Ruth Ross, that challenged the then orthodox position on the Treaty of Waitangi. So, it may be said that while some of the women writers at the time of 1950s and 1960s were at the forefront of social and political change such as Māori and women's rights issues, the fact of who and what was published was still controlled by male writers, editors and publishers.

Chapter 11

Conclusion

This book on women writers between 1945 and 1970 in New Zealand has examined the evidence on whether they were deliberately under-represented and their work trivialised by the male writers and publishers of the time. I contend that I have established such under-representation and trivialisation. However, it is interesting to note that women novelists of the time were treated differently by their male counterparts than women poets. The former were, in the main, ignored in the literary world, while the latter were treated with a mixture of disdain and hostility.

While the evidence I have presented shows that several women novelists and writers of fiction were often highly successful in terms of commercial sales, that this did not translate into respect and acceptance in the literary world, with the exception of Janet Frame, who, due to her particular circumstances and her mentoring by Frank Sargeson, made her the exception to the rule. Apart from authors like Mary Scott and Joyce West, who were both extremely popular and widely read within New Zealand, most of the successful women of the period had very popular and lucrative careers outside New Zealand. The bibliographical appendices I present with this thesis illustrate this in graphic detail.

As previously discussed, it was in 1930 when the anthology *Kowhai Gold* was published, its editor, Quentin Pope, expressed the hope that its contents might serve as the foundation of a New Zealand literature. However, within a few years the anthology was seen as the embodiment of an outmoded tradition of versifying, dominated by female poets. The verses were depicted as sentimental and clichéd, and Curnow characterised it as a 'lamentable anthology [in which] imported insipidities were mixed with puerilities of local origin'. This attitude appears to have been given its first expression in in 1934 with Glover and Milner's small but influential anthology, *New Poems*. Between this and Curnow's anthology of 1945 a 'masculinist' momentum seems to have gathered pace, helped in part by the advent of the Second World War and its aftermath. For around this time a largely male, secular group of younger poets and critics, attracted by Modernist forms and philosophies, became influential.

The career of poet Eileen Duggan can be seen as a key example of the fate of many New Zealand women poets and writers during the period covered by this thesis. Prominent among the poets included in *Kowhai Gold* was Duggan, who until then had a high reputation. Internationally, her poetry continued to be well received, but in New Zealand her standing began to wane, and never recovered. Duggan's subsequent absence from major anthologies was as a result of her own decision, but it was a decision she felt forced to make by the prejudice and animosity she encountered. During the 1920s and the early 1930s, Duggan was beginning to understand the importance of a national literature for New Zealand – an understanding that, ironically, is not dissimilar from that of the nationalist poets who later condemned her work.

In using the example of Duggan from before the beginning of the period under study, there appears to be a progression of negative thought, words and deeds through to the 1970s regarding the treatment of women writers by their male counterparts. Even after 1970 the pattern of omission continued. For example, in 1972 a new self-styled 'revolutionary' poetry periodical began. In first issue of *Lipsync* were '36 New Poems by New Zealand's Leading Writers'. However, of the 25 poets represented only two were women, Joan Shirley-Thompson and Riemke Ensing. The evidence I have presented in the individual chapters of this thesis and the appendices that accompany them show a definite trend, and at times specific deliberate examples, of male indifference and at times malevolence directed towards female subjects, sensibilities and styles of writing as well as individual women writers themselves.

As discussed in the chapter on the literary background to this thesis, it was Curnow's following of T.S. Eliot's 'ban on the personal' that represented a fundamental difference between male and female writing. This became what was essentially a difference between the Georgian and Modernist philosophies of literary thought, with Curnow representing the Modernist school of thought as it manifested itself as an anti-female movement within New Zealand literature. Apreciation of women's writing was to surface in gender-specific feminist publications such as *Broadsheet* together with writing by women academics like Wevers and McLeod. However, the majority of these critiques only appeared after the period covered by my thesis, although Joan Stevens at least mentioned Romance writing in her work, if somewhat disparagingly. In the 1980s critics like Terry Sturm made a reappraisal of some of the women writers such as Rosemary Rees.

I noted in my chapter on Methodology that women were considered Other not because they are numerically less in number than the dominant group, but because of their sex alone. Indeed, one of the objectives of this thesis is to facilitate debate in relation to the women writers of the 1945 to 1970 period in New Zealand and how they might be considered in terms of their Otherness to New Zealand male writers of the time. It is in the words of the women writers themselves that the most compelling evidence can be found. The poet Ruth Gilbert is recorded in a 1967 interview on the male response to women writers:

> I think most male reviewers approach a piece of writing differently when they see a woman's name on it. They unconsciously patronise. A writer wants to be recognised as a writer, not as a man or a woman. But even when a woman writer becomes known, she is not the male writer's equal (Gilbert in 'Sketch' Wright, 2007: 17-18).

It will be remembered that Gilbert wrote of poet and editor Louis Johnson that she would have to change her sex for Johnson to fully accept her as a writer, and Willow Macky suggested that women had felt they had to ape men 'Monkey-like' in order to be taken seriously. Later in the 1960s and 1970s women would take over their own affairs in relation to publishing and promoting their own work. However, even when this happened there seemed little hope of women's work being accepted in mainstream literary annals. Lesbian poet Heather McPherson echoes Gilbert's remarks by recalling the early 1970s. When asked what her place in New Zealand literature might be, she states: 'By the New Zealand literary scene? It could be surprising to be acknowledged at all, given some of the hostile editorialising at the time'. In the 1970s, women writers and artists began to set up their own publishing and distribution.

This attempt at autonomy can be seen in the presses founded during the drive by members of the women's liberation movement to give the new breed of women writers a voice independent of the patriarchy. A question raised by this thesis is the role played by the New Zealand Women Writers' Society in relation to why they did not establish their own publishing house in order to publish and distribute books beyond their 1953 anthology, *POEMS*. Why did they need a 'patron' like Pat Lawlor, why did they need a man to write the forward to their volume? They all appear to be reasonably well off, well educated, middle class women so what stopped them from setting up an autonomous publishing house such as would be the case of women in the 1970s and beyond.

In discussing the factors accounting for the under-representation and trivialization of women writers of my period, I have explored the social and historical context for women, including the impact of WW2, and outlined the careers of a number of women poets and novelists, including some detailed case studies. I have also examined the particular issues facing Māori and lesbian writers. I conclude that a supportive and encouraging environment was rarely available for women writers from 1945 to 1970, that most struggled to be published and appreciated, and that only later, if at all, with the progress of second wave feminism, were many of these important writers properly recognised.

I have throughout used the ideas of inclusion and diversity inherent in my understanding of what was required to reflect both the underlying philosophy of both the feminist methodologies and the Gender and Women's Studies Department. Thus I have used a multitude of concepts and research methods. While this approach may have its limitations of throwing the net too widely, I have from the outset stated that I wanted to provide an overview of the period I had chosen to write on, and to provide a starting point for further study by providing bibliographical and biographical material that may be difficult to otherwise access. If I have achieved this then my work has been well worth the effort.

Thus, this thesis has explored the constraints that delayed and inhibited the work of a gifted generation of women writers, some of whom were recognised in the post-1970s period after second wave had successfully removed some of the barriers to women's full participation in the cultural life of New Zealand. Through examining the detail of selected writers' lives, it is possible to understand how their exclusion was systemic rather than individual, and how the prevailing structures of sexism, racism, classism and homophobia worked to normalise the prototypical great New Zealand writer of the period as invariably male, white, middle-class, and preferably with direct experience of bloody and violent war service that could become significant material for his poetry and prose.

The leading writers, publishers, and critics of the 1945-70 period operated in the shadow of WW2, developing and clinging to attitudes that successfully excluded women writers from the literary canon and it is in this context that binarism is important. The fact that the male writers, publishers and critics, in effect, set up an 'us and them' situation with regard to gender, or more to the point an 'us and don't worry about them' leads to any discussion on the period as being binary by nature.

This thesis has been a long learning curve for me. It has been an honour to work with the many people who have helped me. When I started out I had an idea that, as I have said, grew out of my MA thesis on small press publishing. It has always been my ambition as a writer, artist, publisher, and academic to contribute to the cultural wealth of New Zealand/Aotearoa. I also have a keen feeling for righting injustice, and this was one of the driving forces behind my wanting to investigate the topic chosen. Like all investigations of this nature much of what I found was quite surprising.

One of the most interesting things was the successes of the women novelists of the period. The fact that much of that success was experienced overseas and that women like Ngaio Marsh felt shunned by her homeland is significant. Looking at the bibliographies of Dorothy Eden and Dorothy Quentin gives a great insight into the success of these two novelists. The number of languages they were translated into and their commercial success are all significantly undermined by the lack of critical acclaim here. Dismissed as either 'Crime Writers' or 'Romance Writers', these women were not considered real writers. Even Rosemary Rees described herself in self-deprecating tones as 'the highest paid author in New Zealand' as though it was something to be ashamed of rather than celebrated.

However, it has been the attitudes to women poets of the period that has really made my thesis worthwhile for me. To find out how badly they were treated by their male counterparts was quite shocking. I have over the years had the privilege to work with many women poets, either at poetry readings or in my capacity as a publisher. We have always treated each other with mutual respect and I have always considered their work in the same way I have treated the male poets I have published. Therefore, I hope that this thesis is used as an inspiration for further investigation in more detail about the issues raised and the poets written about in this sketch.

My conclusion to this thesis must be one of regret, that the New Zealand readers were largely denied the pleasure of reading several of these writers until a later period, that New Zealand literature was not influenced by their work until later, and the writers themselves experienced so many hardships and difficulties before their work was recognised, if at all. I conclude this thesis by reference again to 'Judith' Shakespeare. In the words of Virginia Woolf:

> ... Shakespeare had a sister ... she died young – alas! She never wrote a word ... she lives in you and me, and in many other women who are not here tonight, for they are washing up the dishes and putting the children to bed. But she lives; for great poets do not die; they are continuing presences ... the opportunity will come and the dead poet who was Shakespeare's sister will put on the body which she has so often laid down ... when she is born again she shall find it possible to live and write her poetry ... (Woolf, 2000: 148-149).

Select Bibliography

Aitken, Judith. *A Woman's Place: a Study of the Changing Role of Women in New Zealand.* Auckland: Heinemann Educational Books, 1975.

Alley, Elizabeth, ed. *The Inward Sun: Celebrating the Life and Work of Janet Frame.* Wellington: Daphne Brassell Associates Press, 1994.

Anon. *New Zealand Literature: Author's Week 1936, Annals of New Zealand Literature.* Wellington: New Zealand Author's Week Committee, 1936.

Ashcroft, Bill, Gareth Griffiths, and Helen Tiffin. *The Empire Writes Back: Theory and Practice in Post-Colonial Literatures.* London: Routledge, 1989.

Ashton-Warner, Sylvia. *Spinster.* London: Secker & Warburg, 1958.

Bagnall, A.G., P.A. Griffith, and K.S. Williams, eds. *New Zealand National Bibliography: To The Year 1960.* Wellington: Government Printer, 1980.

Barrowman, Rachel. *A Popular Vision: The Arts and the Left in New Zealand 1930-1950.* Wellington: Victoria University Press, 1991.

Baxter, James K. *The Fire and the Anvil.* Wellington: New Zealand University Press, 1957.

Baxter, James K. *The Man on the Horse.* Dunedin: University of Otago Press, 1967.

Baxter, James K. *Autumn Testament.* Wellington: Price Milburn, 1974.

Baysting, Arthur, [ed]. *The Young New Zealand Poets.* Auckland: Heinemann Educational Books, 1973.

Bebbington, W.G. [ed]. *Introducing Modern Poetry: An Anthology.* London: Faber & Faber, 1944.

Bernikow, Louise, [ed]. *The World Split Open: Four Centuries of Women Poets in England and America 1552-1950.* London: The Women's Press, 1974.

Birchfield, Maureen. *Looking for Answers: A Life of Elsie Locke.* Christchurch: Canterbury University Press, 2009.

Blain, Virginia & Isobel Grundy & Patricia Clements, eds. *The Feminist Companion to Literature in English.* New Haven: Yale University Press, 1990.

Bonner, Frances, Lizbeth Goodman, Richard Allen, Linda Janes, and Catherine King, eds. *Imagining Women.* Cambridge, UK: Polity Press, 1995.

Boraman, Toby. *Rabble Rousers and Merry Pranksters: a History of Anarchism in Aotearoa/New Zealand from the Mid 1950s to the Early 1980s.* Christchurch/Wellington: Katipo Books and Irrecuperable Press, 2007.

Bornholdt, Jenny and Gregory O'Brien, [eds]. *My Heart Goes Swimming: New Zealand Love Poems.* Auckland: Godwit, 2000.

Brasch, Charles, [ed]. *Landfall Country: Work from Landfall 1947-61 chosen by Charles Brasch: Stories, Poems, Essays, Paintings.* Christchurch: The Caxton Press, 1962.

Brasch, Charles. *The Universal Dance: A Selection from the Critical Prose Writings of Charles Brasch.* Dunedin: University of Otago Press, 1981.

Brookes, Barbara, Charlotte Macdonald, and Margaret Tennant, eds. *Women in History: Essays on European Women in New Zealand.* Wellington: Allen & Unwin/Port Nicholson Press, 1986.

Broughton, W.S. *A.R.D. Fairburn.* Wellington: A.H. & A.W. Reed, 1968.

Brunton, Alan. *Years Ago Today: Language & Performance: 1969.* Wellington: Bumper Books, 1997.

Brunton, Alan, Murray Edmond, and Michele Leggott, eds. *Big Smoke: New Zealand Poems 1960-1975.* Auckland: Auckland University Press, 2000.

Buck, Claire, ed. *Bloomsbury Guide to Women's Literature.* London: Bloomsbury Publishing, 1992.

Bunkle, Phillida, and Beryl Hughes, eds. *Women in New Zealand Society.* Sydney: Allen & Unwin, 1980.

Burgess, Grace. *A Gentle Poet: A Portrait of Eileen Duggan, O.B.E.* Masterton: Grace Burgess, 1981.

Burns, James. *A Century of New Zealand Novels: A bibliography of the period 1861-1960.* Auckland: Whitcombe & Tombs, 1961.

Burns, James. *New Zealand Novels and Novelists 1861-1979: an Annotated Bibliography.* Auckland: Heinemann Publishers, 1981.

Butterworth, Karen Peterson. *Fluid.* Paekakariki: Earl of Seacliff Art Workshop, 2006.

Cadman, Eileen, Gail Chester, Agnes Pivot. *Rolling Our Own: Women as Printers, Publishers and Distributors.* London: Minority Press Group, 1981.

Campbell, Alistair Te Ariki. *The Dark Lord of Savaiki: Collected Poems.* Christchurch: Hazard Press, 2005.

Campbell, Alistair Te Ariki & Meg Campbell. *It's Love, Isn't It? The Love Poems.* Wellington: HeadworX, 2008.

Campbell, Helen. *Mary Lambie: A Biography.* Wellington: The New Zealand Nursing and Research Foundation, 1976.

Campbell, Meg. *Resistance.* Paekakariki: Earl of Seacliff Art Workshop, 2005.

Caute, David. *Fanon.* London: Fontana/Collins, 1970.

Challis, Derek, and Gloria Rawlinson. *The Book of Iris: A Biography of Robin Hyde.* Auckland: Auckland University Press, 2002.

Chapman, Robert, and Jonathon Bennett, [eds]. *An Anthology of New Zealand Verse.* London: Oxford University Press, 1956.

Clarke, Isabel C. *Katherine Mansfield: a Biography.* Wellington: The Beltane Book Bureau, 1944.

Condliffe, J.B. *The Welfare State in New Zealand.* London: George Allen & Unwin, 1959.

Coney, Sandra, et al, [eds]. *United Women's Convention: Report.* Auckland: W.E.A., 1973.

Coney, Sandra. *Every Girl: A Social History of Women and the YWCA in Auckland.* Auckland: YWCA, 1986.

Coney, Sandra. *Standing in the Sunshine: a History of New Zealand Women Since They Won the Vote.* Auckland: Viking, 1993.

Cox, Shelagh, [ed]. *Public & Private Worlds: Women in Contemporary New Zealand.* Wellington: Allen & Unwin/Port Nicholson Press, 1987.

Curnow, Allen, [ed]. *A Book of New Zealand Verse 1923-1945.* Christchurch: The Caxton Press, 1945.

Curnow, Allen, [ed]. *A Book of New Zealand Verse 1923-1950.* Christchurch: The Caxton Press, 1951.

Curnow, Allen. In R.A.K. Mason, *Collected Poems.* Christchurch: Pegasus Press, 1963.

Curnow, Allen, ed. *The Penguin Book of New Zealand Verse.* Auckland: Penguin Books with Blackwood & Janet Paul, 1966.

Curnow, Allen. *Look Back Harder: Critical Writings 1935-1984*, Peter Simpson, ed. Auckland: AUP, 1987.

Curnow, Wystan, ed. *Essays on New Zealand Literature.* Auckland: Heinemann Educational Books, 1973.

Dallas, Ruth. *Curved Horizon: An Autobiography.* Dunedin: University of Otago Press, 1991.

Dalziel, Margaret. *Janet Frame.* Wellington: Oxford University, 1980.

Dann, Christine. *Up from Under: Women and Liberation in New Zealand 1970-1985.* Wellington: Port Nicholson Press, 1985.

Davin, Dan. *Not Here, Not Now.* Auckland: Whitcombe & Tombs, 1970.

Davin, Dan. *Closing Times.* Auckland: OUP, 1985.

de Beauvoir, S. *The Second Sex.* New York: Alfred Knopf, 1952.de la Mare, Walter. In Eileen Duggan, introduction. *Poems.* London: Allen and Unwin, 1937.

de Montalk, Count Potocki. *Recollections of My Fellow Poets.* Auckland: Prometheus Press, 1983.

Diaz; Angeli R. 'Postcolonial Theory and the Third Wave Agenda.' *Women and Language* Vol. 26, (2003).

Drabble, Margaret, ed. *The Oxford Companion to English Literature.* Oxford: Oxford University Press, 1996.

Drayton, Joanne. *Ngaio Marsh: Her Life in Crime.* Auckland: HarperCollins, 2008.

'Dreams, John, O'', ed. *Gift Book of New Zealand Verse.* Wellington: N.Z. Radio Publishing Company, undated.

Du Chateau, Robyn. In Tolerton, Jane. *60s Chicks hit the nineties.* Auckland: Penguin Books, 1997.

Duggan, Eileen. *Poems.* London: Allen & Unwin, 1937.

Duggan, Eileen. *More Poems.* London: Allen & Unwin, 1951.

Dunlop, Alan R., ed. *Poems: Anthology by New Zealand Women Writers.* Invercargill: New Zealand Women Writers and Artists' Society, 1953.

Eagleton, Terry. *Marxism and Literary Critism.* London: Methuen & Co, 1985.

Edmond, Lauris, ed. *Women in Wartime: New Zealand Women Tell Their Story.* Wellington: Government Printing Office Publishing, 1986.

Edwards, Brian. *Helen: Portrait of a Prime Minister.* Auckland: Exisle Publishing, 2001.

Edwards, Mihi. *Mihipeka: Early Years.* Auckland: Penguin Books, 1990.

Eldred-Grigg, Stevan. *Blue Blood.* Auckland: Penguin Books, 1997.

Ell, Sarah, ed. *The Lives of Pioneer Women in New Zealand: From Their Letters, Diaries and Reminiscences.* Auckland: The Bush Press, 1993.

Else, Anne, ed. *Women Together: A History of Women's Organisations in New Zealand, Ngā Ropū Wāhine ō te Motu.* Wellington: Historical Branch, Department of Internal Affairs, Daphne Brasell Associates Press, 1993.

Ensing, Riemke, ed. *Private Gardens: An Anthology of New Zealand Women Poets.* Dunedin: Caveman Press, 1977.

Evans, Marian, Bridie Lonie, and Tilly Lloyd, eds. *A Women's Picture Book: 25 Women Artists of Aotearoa (New Zealand).* Wellington: GP Books, 1988.

Evans, Patrick. *The Penguin History of New Zealand Literature.* Auckland: Penguin Books, 1990.

Evans, Patrick. *The Long Forgetting: Post-colonial literary culture in New Zealand.* Christchurch: Canterbury University Press, 2007.

Fairburn, A.R.D. *The Woman Problem and Other Prose.* Auckland: Paul, 1967.

Fairburn, A.R.D. *Collected Poems.* Christchurch: Pegasus Press, 1967.

Faludi, Susan. *Backlash: the Undeclared War Against Women.* London: Chatto & Windus, 1992.

Forster, John, ed. *Social Process in New Zealand: Readings in Sociology.* Auckland: Longman Paul, 1969.

Frame, Janet. *Janet Frame: An Autobiography.* Auckland: Random Century, 1991.

Frame, Janet. *Toward Another Summer.* Auckland: Vintage, 2007.

Frame, Janet. *Faces in the Water.* London: Virago Modern Classics, 2009.

France, Thelma, Hestia Quinn, Roma Henden, and Isobelle Ashforht, eds. *History of New Zealand Women Writers' Society 1932-1982.* Wellington: New Zealand Women Writers' Society, 1982.

Fyfe, Judith, ed. *Matriarchs: A Generation of New Zealand Women Talk to Judith Fyfe.* Auckland: Penguin Books, 1990.

Gamman, Lorraine, and Margaret Marshment, eds. *The Female Gaze: Women as Viewers of Popular Culture.* Seattle: The Real Comet Press, 1989.

Gibbs, Rowan. *Dorothy Quentin: A La Recherche De La Madeleine Perdue: a Bibliographical Romance.* Te Aro, Wellington: Original Books, 2005.

Gilbert, Ruth. *Collected Poems.* Wellington: Black Robin, 1984.

Gilbert, Ruth. *Early Poems: 1938-1944.* Wellington: Cultural and Political Booklets, 1988.

Glover, Denis & Ian Milner, eds. *New Poems.* [Christchurch]: The Caxton Club Press, 1934.

Glover, Denis. *Hot Water Sailor and Landlubber Ho!* Auckland: Collins, 1981.

Glover, Denis. *Selected Poems.* Auckland: Penguin, 1981.

Glover, Rupert, ed. *Strawberry Fields: Arts Festival Poetry Yearbook.* Christchurch: University of Canterbury Students' Association, 1967.

Gluck, Shema Berger. *Rosie the Riveter Revisited: Women, the War and Social Change.* New York: Meridian/New American Library, 1988.

Goldin, Claudia. *Understanding the Gender Gap: An Economic History of American Women.* New York: Oxford University Press, 1990.

Griffith, Penelope, Peter Hughes & Alan Loney eds. *A Book in the Hand.* Auckland: Auckland University Press, 2000.

Hayward, Margaret & Joy Cowley, eds. *Women Writers of New Zealand 1932-1982.* Wellington: N.Z. Women Writers' Society/Colonial Associates, 1982.

Heilbrun, Carolyn G. *Writing a Woman's Life.* New York: W.W. Norton, 1988.

Heim, Otto. *Writing Along Broken Lines: Violence and Ethnicity in Contemporary Māori Fiction.* Auckland: Auckland University Press, 1998.

Hilliard, Chris. *The Bookman's Dominion: Cultural Life in New Zealand 1920-1950.* Auckland: Auckland University Press, 2006.

Holcroft, M.H. *Reluctant Editor: the Listener Years, 1949-1967.* Wellington: Reed, 1969.

Holcroft, M.H. *Mary Ursula Bethell.* Wellington: Oxford University Press, 1975.

Hood, Lynley. *Sylvia!: The Biography of Sylvia Ashton-Warner.* Auckland: Viking, 1988.

Hughes, Beryl, and Sheila Ahern. *Redbrick and Bluestockings: Women at Victoria 1899-1993*. Wellington: Victoria University Press, 1993.

Hyde, Robin. *Journalese*. Auckland: The National Printing Co. Ltd., 1934.

Hyman, Prue. *Women and Economics: a New Zealand Feminist Perspective*. Wellington: Bridget Williams Books, 1994.

James, Bev & Kay Saville-Smith. *Gender, Culture & Power*. Auckland: Oxford University Press, 1994.

Jensen, Kai. *Whole Men: the Masculinist Tradition in New Zealand Literature*. Auckland: Auckland University Press, 1996.

Johnson, Louis, ed. 'numbers seven'. Wellington: Literary Review: 1957, p28.

Johnson, Olive. *A.R.D. Fairburn, 1904-1957, A Bibliography of his Published Work*. Auckland: Auckland University Monograph Series No. 3, 1958.

Jones, Alison. 'Writing Feminist Educational Research: Am 'I' in the text.' In *Women and Education in Aotearoa 2*, edited by Sue Middleton and Alison Jones. Wellington: Bridget Williams Books, 1992.

Kessler-Harris, Alice. *A Woman's Wage: Historical Meanings and Social Consequences*. Lexington: University Press of Kentucky, 1990.

King, Michael. *Wrestling with the Angel: a Life of Janet Frame*. Auckland: Viking, 2000.

King, Michael. *The Penguin History of New Zealand*. Auckland: Viking, 2004.

Laurie, Alison J., ed. *Lesbian Studies in Aotearoa/New Zealand*. New York: Harrington Park Press, 2001.

Lennon, John and Yoko Ono. *Sometime in New York City*. London: Apple, 1972.

Letherby, Gayle. *Feminist Research in Theory and Practice*. Philadelphia: Open University Press, 2003.

Lewis, Margaret. *Ngaio Marsh: A Life*. Wellington: Bridget Williams Books, 1991.

Locke, Terry, [ed]. *Jewels in the Water: Contemporary New Zealand poetry for younger readers*. Hamilton: Leaders Press, 2000.

Locke, Terry, ed. *Doors: a Contemporary New Zealand Poetry Selection*. Hamilton: Leaders Press, 2000.

Lovell-Smith, Margaret, ed. *The Woman Question: Writings by the Women who Won the Vote*. Auckland: New Women's Press, 1992.

Macdonald, Charlotte, Merimeri Penfold, Bridget Williams, eds. *The Book of New Zealand Women: Ko Kui Ma Te Kaupapa*. Wellington: Bridget Williams Books, 1992.

MacKay, Jessie. *Land of the Morning*. Christchurch: Whitcombe and Tombs, 1909.

Mackersey, Ian. *Jean Batten: The Garbo of the Skies*. Auckland: Macdonald Publishers (New Zealand) Ltd, 1990.

Marris, C.A., ed. *New Zealand Best Poems*. Wellington: Harry H. Tombs, 1933 to 1941.

Marsh, Ngaio. *Black Beech and Honeydew: An Autobiography*. London: Collins, 1966.

Mason, Bruce. *New Zealand Drama: A Parade of Forms and a History*. Wellington: New Zealand University Press, 1973.

Maynard, Mary and June Purvis, eds. *Researching Women's Lives from a Feminist Perspective*. London: Taylor & Francis, 1994.

McAlpine, Rachel, ed. *The Passionate Pen: New Zealand's Romance Writers talk to Rachel McAlpine*. Christchurch: Hazard Press, 1998.

McCahon, Colin. *Rita: Seven Poems by Colin McCahon*. Wellington/Auckland: Fernbank Studio/The Holloway Press, 2001.

McGregor, Rae. *The Story of a New Zealand writer: Jane Mander*. Dunedin: University of Otago Press, 1998.

McKay, Frank. *New Zealand Poetry: An introduction through the discussion of selected poems*. Wellington: New Zealand University Press/Price Milburn, 1970.

McLeod, Aorewa, ed. *New Women's Fiction*. Auckland: New Women's Press, 1988.

McNaughton, Trudie, ed. *In Deadly Earnest: A Collection of Fiction by New Zealand Women 1870s-1980s*. Auckland: Century Hutchinson, 1989.

McPherson, Heather. *Travel and other compulsions*. Paekakariki: Earl of Seacliff Art Workshop, 2004.

McQueen, Harvey. *The New Place*. Wellington: Victoria University Press, 1993.

Meikle, Phoebe. *Accidental Life*. Auckland: Auckland University Press, 1994.

Mitcalfe, Barry. *Poetry of the Māori: (translations)*. Hamilton: Paul's Book Arcade, 1961.

Morris, Paul, Harry Rickets and Mike Grimshaw, eds. 'Spirit Abroad: A Second Anthology of New Zealand Spiritual Verse'. Auckland: Godwit/RandomHouse, 2004.

Mulgan, Alan. *Literature and Authorship in New Zealand*. London: George Allen & Unwin Ltd, 1943.

Mulgan, Alan. *Great Days in New Zealand Writing*. Wellington: A.H. & A.W. Reed, 1962.

Murphy, Rosalie, ed: with a pref. by C. Day Lewis. *Contemporary Poets of the English Language*. Chicago: St. James Press, 1970.

Murray, Stuart. *Never a Soul at Home: New Zealand Literary Nationalism and the 1930s*. Wellington: Victoria University Press, 1998.

Myers, Virginia. *Head & Shoulders: Successful New Zealand Women Talk to Virginia Myers*. Auckland: Penguin Books, 1987.

Nicholls, Marjory Lydia. *A Venture in Verse*. Wellington: Whitcombe and Tombs, 1917.

Nicholls, Marjory Lydia. *Gathered Leaves*. Wellington: Whitcombe and Tombs, 1922.

Nicholls, Marjory Lydia. *Thirdly*. Wellington: [Private, Harry H Tombs, 1929/30].

Nolan, Melanie. *Bread Winning: New Zealand women and the state*. Christchurch: Canterbury University Press, 2000.

O'Brien, Gregory. *A Nest of Singing Birds: 100 Years of the New Zealand School Journal*. Wellington: Learning Media, 2007.

O'Donnell, Margaret J, ed. *Anthology of Commonwealth Verse*. London: Blackie, 1963.

O'Leary, Michael, ed. *Wrapper*. Seacliff: Earl of Seacliff Art Workshop, 1992.

O'Leary, Michael. *Alternative Small Press Publishing in New Zealand: an Introduction, with Particular Reference to the Years 1969-1999*. Wellington: Steele Roberts, 2007.

Oliver, W.H. *Poetry in New Zealand*. Wellington: School Publications Branch, Department of Education, 1960.

Oliver, W.H. *Looking for the Phoenix: a memoir*. Wellington: Bridget Williams Books, 2002.

Ono, Yoko. *Sometime in New York City*. London: Apple, 1972.

Orbell, Margaret, ed. *Contemporary Māori Writing*. Wellington: A.H. & A.W. Reed, 1974.

O'Sullivan, Vincent, ed. *An Anthology of Twentieth-Century New Zealand Poetry*. London: Oxford University Press, 1970.

O'Sullivan, Vincent. *New Zealand Poetry in the Sixties*. Wellington: School Publications Branch, Department of Education, 1973.

Park, Iris M. *New Zealand Periodicals of Literary Interest*. Wellington: National Library Service, 1962.

Paterson, Alistair, ed. *15 Contemporary New Zealand Poets*. Dunedin: Pilgrims South Press, 1980.

Pewhairangi, Ngoi. *Tuini: Her Life and Her Songs*. Gisborne: Te Rau Press, 1985.

Phillips, Jock. *A Man's Country? The Image of the Pākehā Male, A History*. Auckland: Penguin Books, 1996.

Pirie, Mark, ed. *The Earl is in ... 25 Years of the Earl of Seacliff*. Paekakariki: Earl of Seacliff Art Workshop, 2009.

Pope, Quentin, ed. *Kowhai Gold: An Anthology of Contemporary New Zealand Verse*. London: J.M. Dent, 1930.

Proctor, Ellen A. *A Brief Memoir of Christina G. Rossetti*. London: S.P.C.K., 1895.

Radway, Janice. *Reading the Romance*. North Carolina: The University of North Carolina Press, 1984.

Reeves, James, ed. *Georgian Poetry*. Harmondsworth: Penguin Books, 1962.

Reid, J.C. *Creative Writing in New Zealand: A Brief Critical History*. Auckland: Whitcombe and Tombs, 1946.

Reinharz, Shulamit, with Lynn Davidman. *Feminist Methods in Social Research*. New York: Oxford University Press, 1992.

Rhodes, H. Winston and Denis Glover, [eds.] *Verse Alive: number* two. Christchurch: The Caxton Press, 1937.

Rich, Adrienne. *Diving into the Wreck: Poems 1971-1972*. New York: W.W. Norton, 1973.

Rich, Adrienne. *What is Found There: Notebooks on Poetry and Politics*. New York, W.W. Norton & Company, 2003.

Richmond, Mary E. *Late Harvest*. Te Aro, Wellington: Original Books, 2007.

Roberts, Helen, ed. *Doing Feminist Research*. London: Routledge & Kegan Paul, 1982.

Robinson, Roger, and Nelson Wattie, eds. *The Oxford Companion to New Zealand Literature*. Auckland: Oxford University Press, 1998.

Rowbotham, Sheila. *Hidden from History: 300 Years of Women's Oppression and the Fight Against It.* London: Pluto Press, 1974.

Rupp, Leila J. *Mobilizing Women for War: German and American Propaganda, 1939-1945.* Princeton: Princeton University Press, 1978.

Russ, Joanna. *How to Suppress Women's Writing.* London: The Women's Press, 1984.

Said, E. *Orientalism.* London: Routledge & Kegan Paul, 1978.

Sargeson, Frank. *Sargeson.* Auckland: Penguin, 1981.

Sargison, Patricia A. *Victoria's Furthest Daughters: A bibliography of published sources for the study of women in New Zealand 1830-1914.* Wellington: Alexander Turnbull Library Endowment Trust with the New Zealand Founders Society, 1984.

Saul, Jennifer. *Feminism: Issues and Arguments.* New York: Oxford University Press, 2003.

Shaw, Helen [guest editor, International ed; associate editor, Sandra Fowler; editor, Amal Ghose]. *The Japonica sings: Ocarina's Anthology of New Zealand and World Poetry.* Madras: Ocarina International, 1979.

Shaw, Helen, ed. *Mystical Choice: 47 poems by New Zealand poets.* Auckland: Mandala Editions, 1981.

Shepard, Deborah, ed. *Between the Lives: Partners in Art.* Auckland: Auckland University Press, 2005.

Showalter, Elaine, ed. *The New Feminist Criticism: Essays on Women, Literature, and Theory.* New York: Pantheon Books, 1985.

Smith, E.M. *A History of New Zealand Fiction.* Dunedin & Wellington: A.H. & A.W. Reed, 1939.

Smithyman, Kendrick. *A Way of Saying: A Study of New Zealand Poetry.* Auckland: Collins, 1965.

Stafford, Jane & Mark Williams. *Maoriland: New Zealand Literature 1872-1914.* Wellington: Victoria University Press, 2006.

Stanley, Liz & Sue Wise, eds. *Breaking Out Again: Feminist Ontology and Epistemology.* Oxford, UK: Routledge, 1993.

Stead, C.K. *New Zealand Short Stories: Second Series.* Auckland: Oxford University Press, 1966.

Stead, C.K. *In the Glass Case: Essays on New Zealand Literature.* Auckland: Auckland University Press with Oxford University Press, 1981.

Stead, C.K. *Answering to the Language: Essays on Modern Writers.* Auckland: Auckland University Press, 1989.

Steeds, Bernie. 'Mysterious double Life of Dame Ngaio Marsh.' *Evening Post,* April 15 1995.

Stein, Gertrude. *Lectures in America.* London: Virago Press, 1988.

Stevens, Joan. *Some Nineteenth Century Novels and their First Publication.* Wellington: Government Printer, 1961.

Stevens, Joan. *The New Zealand Novel 1860-1965.* Wellington: Reed, 1966.

Sturm, J.C. *Dedications.* Wellington: Steele Roberts, 1996.

Sturm, J.C. *Postscripts.* Wellington: Steele Roberts, 2000.

Sturm, J.C. *House of the Talking Cat.* Wellington: Steele Roberts, 2003.

Sturm, Terry, ed. *The Oxford History of New Zealand Literature in English.* Auckland: Oxford University Press, 1998.

Thomson, John N, ed. *Five New Zealand Plays.* Auckland: Collins Publishers, 1962.

Thwaite, J.L. *The importance of being Eve Langley.* Sydney: Angus & Robertson, 1989.

Tod, Frank. *The History of Seacliff.* [Seacliff: Private Publication, c1970.]

Todd, Janet, ed. *Gender and Literary Voice.* New York: Holmes & Meier Publishers, 1980.

Tolerton, Jane. *60s Chicks hit the nineties.* Auckland: Penguin Books, 1997.

Tong, Rosemary. *Feminist Thought: a more comprehensive introduction [2nd Ed].* Colorado: Westview Press, 1998.

Torrey, E. Fuller. *The Roots of Treason: Ezra Pound and the Secrets of St Elizabeth's.* London: Sidgwick & Jackson, 1984.

Trussell, Denys. *Fairburn.* Auckland: AUP/OUP, 1984.

Tupuola, Anne-Marie, et al, eds. *Ehara i a Koe Anake: You're Not Alone: A Collection of Young Women's Writing.* Wellington: Y.W.C.A., 2000.

Webby, Elizabeth and Lydia Wevers, eds. *Goodbye to Romance: Stories by New Zealand and Australian Women Writers 1930-1988.* Wellington: Allen & Unwin in association with Port Nicholson Press, 1989.

Wedde, Ian & Harvey McQueen [eds]. *Penguin Book of New Zealand Verse*. Auckland: Penguin, 1985.

Whiteford, Peter, ed. *Eileen Duggan: Selected Poems*. Wellington: Victoria University Press, 1994.

Wilson, Guthrie. *Brave Company*. Auckland: Paul's Book Arcade, 1962.

Woolf, Virginia. *The Common Reader*. London: The Hogarth Press, 1957.

Woolf, Virginia. *A Room of One's Own*. Oxford, UK: Oxford University Press, 2000.

Wordsworth, Jane. *Leading Ladies: Twenty-three Outstanding Women*. Wellington: A.H. & A.W. Reed, 1979.

Wright, Dr. F.W. Nielsen. *A Checklist of Anthologies and Critical Books etc. Published in 1945-1970 Regarding Aotearoa Poetry*. Te Aro, Wellington: Cultural and Political Booklets, 2007.

www.ingramcontent.com/pod-product-compliance
Lightning Source LLC
Chambersburg PA
CBHW050537280326
41933CB00011B/1619